Dancing in the Movies

The Iowa School of Letters

Award for Short Fiction

Prize money for the award is provided by

a grant from the Iowa Arts Council

Dancing in the Movies

ROBERT BOSWELL

UNIVERSITY OF IOWA PRESS

IOWA CITY

"The Right Thing" first appeared in
The Antioch Review.
"Dancing in the Movies" first appeared in
TriQuarterly, a publication of Northwestern University.
"Little Bear" first appeared in *Passages North.*
"The Darkness of Love" first appeared in *Ploughshares.*

Library of Congress Cataloging in Publication Data

Boswell, Robert, 1953–

Dancing in the movies.

Contents: Little bear—Kentucky—Dancing in
the movies—[etc.]

I. Title.

PS3552.O8126D3   1986   813'.54   85-13966
ISBN 0-87745-134-6

University of Iowa Press, Iowa City 52242

Printed in the United States of America

First edition, 1986

Jacket and book design by Richard Hendel

Typesetting by G&S Typesetters, Inc., Austin, Texas

Printing and binding by Thomson-Shore, Inc., Dexter, Michigan

FOR TONI

Contents

Little Bear

Joey Malone found Pfc Owens under a transport truck.

"You getting overtime?" Joey said.

Owens scooted out on his back. He held a black radiator hose in his hand. "They said it needed a new radiator. Look here." He bent the rubber hose to expose a crack. "I been lying under there a half hour thinking how stupid the army is."

He stood, skinny and black, threw the hose in a metal barrel, blew into his cupped hands. "Colder than Bejesus," he said.

Joey nodded. He looked out over the support unit and beyond it to the gray Korean landscape. When Joey had first joined the unit, the pointy canvas tents and six-wheel trucks, the single-axle trailers and barking officers had reminded him of the circus that came to Michigan City in the spring, setting up in a field near the prison. Now, he could see only trucks, trailers, and temporary quarters.

Joey stuck his hands inside his jacket, under his arms. "Sergeant Anderson said I'm ready."

Owens stomped his feet to fight the cold. "I'm staying," he said.

Joey and Owens were the last of Master Sergeant Anderson's training detail, organized to make men who had performed badly in combat ready to return. Owens, they had discovered, was a good mechanic, so good he would stay with the support unit indefinitely. He had tried to teach Joey, telling him to picture the engine running, the pistons shooting in and out like the legs of chorus girls they'd seen in a camp movie. Joey couldn't see it. His head was too full of army regulations and meaningless numbers, images of Indiana and a great blank fear of dying. He would have to return to combat.

"I have to report to him in an hour," Joey said. "He wants to *talk* to me."

"That's lousy, Joey. I'd take combat over that." Owens pulled a cigarette from his pocket, lit it, and inhaled deeply. "Luckily, I don't have to do neither. You, on the other hand . . ." Owens chuckled.

Joey laughed with him. "I, on the other hand, get screwed coming and going."

Owens laughed, spitting out his cigarette. "That's the looks of it." He picked the white butt off the ground and blew on it. The end glowed orange. He twisted dirt off the lip end. "My last cigarette," he said, looked it over again, and tossed it back to the dirt. "This very earth is swarming with bacterias, I bet." He wiped the tips of his fingers against his chest. "Probably a thousand on your shirt alone." He pointed at Joey.

A circle of dirt marked Joey's chest like a target. He wiped and slapped at the dirt. Sergeant Anderson had had him shooting at burning barrels from a ditch as part of his training.

"It's like I slid into home," Joey said.

"Always slide feet first." Owens took two steps, slid into the rear tire of the transport truck. "Feet first." He kicked the tire. "I stole fourteen bases once. In one game."

Joey had been a second baseman in high school, then a shortstop in Okinawa. "There was something I wanted to talk about," Joey said. "Really, something I want to tell you about."

"Michigan City?" Owens said. He was from Brawley, California; Joey from Michigan City, Indiana. They took turns telling about home. "Let's get out of the cold."

They crawled into the cab of the truck. "I've been having dreams about this," Joey said. "It was when I was a kid." His words fogged the windshield.

"Yeah?" Owens said. He blew into his hands again, clapped against his shoulders, rubbed his arms.

"I was ten," Joey said. "My brother was six."

"My brother's six," Owens said, glad to have a connection to the story.

"Nineteen forty-three, I remember that," Joey said. Eight years ago, walking to his friend's house on a street without lights, a night without a moon, Joey had tried to avoid the puddles. His little brother sloshed through them. *What's the point of wearing rubbers if you don't have any fun?* his brother, Dave, said. *Galoshes*, Joey said, *call them galoshes*.

His brother shrugged, said, *Not what Mom calls them.* Joey shook his head. *Trust me,* he said.

Shelling sounded in the distance. Not really like thunder, Joey thought, louder, more explicit. To Owens, he said, "We spent the night at my best friend's house. Mickey Lawanda. His parents were out of town."

"Your folks let you do that? Mine would never. Not when I was ten." Owens slipped his hands under his legs to warm them.

"They didn't know Mickey's parents were gone. He lived across from the penitentiary." Three boys had huddled around the coffee table, reading newspaper clippings aloud to Joey's little brother, who couldn't read. They arranged the clippings in chronological order, passed around the seven pictures the newspaper had run again and again—blood on the tiled floor, the floral wallpaper, the bedspread, the ceiling, and Tomás "Pato" Rodríguez staring into the camera, his hands cupped over his ears.

"This guy, Pato Rodríguez, had killed his girlfriend with scissors," Joey said.

"Crude," Owens said.

"At least, they said he did. He didn't look like a bad guy."

His body had been no larger than a boy's, thin arms thickening at the elbows like the joints of tree limbs. Even in the grainy newspaper photographs, his brown skin looked soft. He couldn't speak English, which had seemed like crime enough. The boys didn't know what Pato meant or why he was called that, but they imagined it meant Tiger or The Knife. Mickey gave each of them nicknames. He labeled Joey "Mongoose" Malone. He called Joey's brother "The Spot" because of the large birthmark that covered part of his jaw and neck. He called himself Mickey "The Wonder" Lawanda. Joey's little brother's name had stuck. Everyone but family called him Spot Malone. Because of that night, Joey thought, because of Pato Rodríguez.

"We read the newspaper stories about the killing. We were

right across from the prison," Joey said and crossed his arms against the cold.

As midnight approached, they stared through the small squares of glass at the prison, a hulking concrete box, dark against the dark sky. Mickey had said it looked like a devil's food cake with barbed wire icing.

"We turned on every light in the house."

His brother had run upstairs, turning on the lights in the bedrooms, hall. Joey covered the downstairs, turning on the lights in the kitchen, closets, dining and living rooms. Mickey went to the cellar, switched on the remaining lights. Joey ran out the front door, a misting rain covering his face, to be sure they had not missed a room. The house had become an island of light.

"What for?" Owens said. "Why the lights?"

"I'm getting to it," Joey said. "We all looked at the pictures from the newspaper one last time." Blood on the tiled floor, blood on the floral wallpaper, blood on the bedspread, blood on the ceiling. "We sat in the front room." They sat separately, each with his back erect, hands palm down on the arms of a chair.

"When they executed Pato," Joey said, "the lights in Mickey's house went dim." Two minutes after midnight, the state of Indiana pumped light through the arteries of Pato Rodríguez. Three boys sat in straight-backed chairs with irretrievable smiles until the few dim moments passed and the lights surged on again.

"What'd it feel like?" Owens said.

The windshield was fogged over. *With my words*, Joey thought, imagining that the story could be read there if you knew how to do it. "It was thrilling," Joey said. *It was frightening. It was terrible, beautiful.*

Nearby, a jeep started up, idled. Owens pulled his knees to his chest, wrapped his arms around them. "Think our deaths here would entertain anybody?"

Joey shrugged.

"Idiots and dogs," Sergeant Anderson said, spitting into a pool of motor oil as they walked to the jeep. "Korea's full of them." Anderson jumped behind the wheel. Joey got in beside him, looked over his shoulder at Owens next to another jeep, oil pan in his hands.

"Every war is just like this." Sergeant Anderson maneuvered the jeep around a puddle of muddy water. "A shithouse mess." He began talking about World War II, how the units were segregated. Joey found he could let the noise of the jeep drown out the words. Owens' regiment had been segregated. They were the last all-Negro unit, broken up after they had bugged out. Owens said the unit joke was that they were the asphalt crew because the army wanted to pave the way to Korea with black asses.

The jeep bounced hard. Mud sprayed from both sides. "Mud'll be ice by midnight," Sergeant Anderson said. "Whole country'll be ice in a week." Joey nodded at the sergeant. "Look here." Anderson switched on the headlights, although the afternoon was still light. He pointed to the road in front of them. "A man's got direction, it's like he's got an extra arm. Army's built-in direction, like what bats got—your own personal radar. *You* can see that, Malone. *You* listen. Most the idiots here never listen to anything but mess call and the sound of money leaving their pockets. That Owens," he threw his thumb back over his shoulder, "wouldn't listen to his own black mother."

Joey followed Anderson's thumb back, half expecting Owens to be there. Korean children sat on a thin gray mattress, stuffing hanging out of it like intestines. "Owens is all right," he said and felt a rush of panic.

Anderson gripped the steering wheel with both hands, switched off the lights, accelerated. The jeep gobbled up the road faster and faster. Anderson's face, Joey realized, was light green, like the meat of a cucumber. The jeep swerved away from a spotted, yapping dog, but the rear wheel caught it. A crack, as if they'd run over a tree limb, and a short whistle.

"Shit," Anderson said. "We kill it?"

The dog's head rose and fell slowly, rose and fell, like a toy dog in the rear window of a car. "Dying," Joey said.

"My brother hit a dog once in Italy," Anderson said.

Joey waited, but Anderson didn't add to the story. The dog's head finally dropped and stayed down, a dark lump on the road. The jeep continued. The sky, in a haze of dust from the jeep, turned khaki.

Half an hour later, the jeep stopped at a windowless, bare plank building just off the side of the road. Over the door hung a yellow sign with red letters: SUZIES SALOON. "Place is a pigsty. But so is all of Korea," Anderson said as he got out of the jeep. Squat, with hunched shoulders, a thick neck, and arms too short for his body, Sergeant Anderson reminded Joey of a giant amphibian.

Anderson shoved a drunken private who blocked the door. Although the ceiling was low, the building had the feeling of a barn. Joey could have turned it into an Indiana barn if not for all the GI's crowding around wooden tables. Sergeant Anderson commandeered a table next to the wall. He grabbed a Korean woman by the thigh. "Get us two beers." He smiled at Joey as the woman walked away. "One time I was a kid and wouldn't eat my string beans. Hated them. My father stuck a revolver to my head and told me to clean my plate. Your father still living?"

"Yes, sir."

"I was mad at him, but I thought, hell, he's my father. My brother Paul come in saying, 'He's a son of a bitch.'" Anderson folded his arms. "We both enlisted young." He leaned against the table. "World War II, Paul and I spent a lot of time in Italy. Got more pussy there than we ever dreamed of in the States." He reached across the table, cupped his hand around Joey's neck, pulled him slightly closer, then let him go. "Got a girl-friend back home—where is it—Michigan?"

"Michigan City, Indiana."

"Got one?"

"No, sir."

"Good. Man don't need a skirt home fucking the plumber while he's gone."

Joey nodded, stared at the table. He felt uneasy, threatened, wondering if this was part of combat training, if he might have to fight a table of drunks or make a weapon out of bottle caps and spit.

The Korean woman returned. Sergeant Anderson paid for the beers. "Completed the training, Malone. Another day or two we're going to join a unit at the front. The both of us. You're a soldier." He reached across the table. Joey took his hand. Anderson gripped it firmly, looked it over. "Important to know a man's hands," he said. They shook, then drank to Joey's accomplishment, the army, Anderson's brother, who had died in North Africa.

"Best beer in the world is in PI. San Miguel. Ever get the chance, go to PI. Heaven for a man."

Joey drank the beer, pretended to be interested. He thought he should ask what PI stood for or whether San Miguel was a place or a beer. He said nothing. The whole evening seemed like a test.

"Basically, I don't like women," Anderson said. "They want you to think you can't live without them. There's a lot you can live without. Sex though." He ran his thumb and forefinger across the end of his nose. "The thing about sex is you can't remember it. You remember the woman, the night, maybe how everything worked up to it. But sex itself can't be remembered. Like a shock or one of those dreams that never come back."

After an hour of drinking and talking, Anderson bought each of them a whore. Joey didn't want one. The sergeant said it was an order. "Next hole you'll be in won't be as warm as this one," he said and shoved a girl at Joey. "She's Suzie," he said, "all the whores are Suzie."

Joey took her hand, followed her through the bar and out a back door. Behind the building, a row of stalls stood like booths at the county fair. A cloth curtain covered the doorway. Inside, a dirt floor, a canvas ceiling ripped open into a smile.

Joey's whore was young and thin and wore a tomato red dress with white buttons the size of quarters. She lit a kerosene lamp. "Cold," she said.

Joey nodded, blew into his hands, shoved them into his pockets.

She unbuttoned the top two buttons, pulled the dress over her head. Her breasts barely lipped away from her chest. She sat on a regulation army cot, smiled up at him with crooked teeth. She said her name was Suzie, then pulled his pants down to his knees. In the cold, his testicles and penis looked like nothing more than a shriveled apricot and stem.

Joey watched the crooked teeth surround his penis, looked above her at the wall, bare except for an ill-framed still life of cabbage and celery. He looked above that, through the tear in the canvas ceiling to the sky. He'd had sex only once before. He began thinking of that night so his penis would get hard.

He had made love with June Norris on the outfield grass in the school ball park one night just before graduation. He remembered the sensation of being inside someone else, and afterward, while he still lay on top of her, she lifted her right arm into the air, pointed to the sky, and said, "Ursa Minor, the Little Bear."

Joey rolled off her, looked up at the stars. She pointed out Little Bear, and squinting his eyes he thought he could picture a bear cub. They lay on the grass and she pointed out other animals in the sky—a bull, a ram. The only one Joey could picture was the bear. June giggled, pulled her checkered dress, which was already pushed up to her chest, over her head. Joey ran his hands over her headless body. She pulled the dress back, bunched it around her neck. Joey thought her head looked like a bean, her lips a hilum. When he told her, she laughed, said he should plant the bean so she could grow another body.

June took his penis, rolled it back and forth in her hands like a child playing with clay. He remembered thinking she was beautiful but never telling her. She said that she was leaving Michigan City to be free, that everyone in the city was in prison whether they knew it or not. She was going to college in the West where not one person in the entire state knew her name. She had promised to write, but Joey never got a single letter. He thought if he were to write her now he'd say, "Suzie was nothing like you."

Anderson talked the whole drive back about being stationed in Italy, how his brother had bought him his first whore. Joey tried to listen, but his mind was in Indiana with his own brother, his father, even his mother, who had been dead for years. Joey was thirteen when his mother was killed crossing Water Street. In his last letter, his father had said the state was going to build a bridge over Water Street. This seemed to make him very happy. His father taught science in high school: the way a cell divides, the position of the earth in the universe. He had majored in English at the University of Indiana, but never taught anything except science. Joey's brother was beginning high school even though he still couldn't read. They'd just kept passing him because his father was a teacher and because he was a good shortstop.

Joey had played shortstop in Okinawa. He had been a shipping clerk and played for the Green Foxes, one of the regiment's teams. Numbers had given him no trouble then. He'd even kept batting averages. During his first few days in Korea, his sense of numbers had suddenly become confused. Fatigue, someone had told him, he would get over it. Instead, it had gotten worse. His head was as much a jumble of meaningless numbers as the bingo cage at the Michigan City Methodist Church.

In the middle of the summer, his battalion had been told

they were being shipped from Okinawa to mainland Japan for six weeks of combat training. In the ship, they were told they would go to Pusan, Korea, for three days of intensive training. When they arrived in Pusan, they were sent to Chinju and combat.

Joey and the Green Foxes' first baseman lugged a .50-caliber machine gun into position to provide cover for the other men. Neither had ever fired a machine gun. Joey was given quick instructions. He followed them, but the gun wouldn't fire. Grease coated his hands and forearms as he went through the steps over and over. The clatter of weapons became more regular, louder. They could not get the gun to fire. Nearby, a corporal shouted coordinates into a radio again and again, then slammed it with his fist. U.S. planes flew overhead, unaware. The radio man stood, screamed numbers at the planes until his face exploded from a round of fire. Joey and the first baseman ran. Joey ran faster. When the first baseman was hit, he called out, "Cinnamon."

Joey wrote to his father that he'd escaped with just some shrapnel in his arm. When the medic dug the fragments out, they were pieces of skull. Joey couldn't finish the letter. Later, he found out the grease was packing grease and the machine gun wouldn't have fired for anyone. By that time, his head was a bingo cage. Since then Joey had been shuffled around Korea like the extra ace in a marked deck, until finally he'd been assigned for special training.

Back from SUZIES SALOON, asleep in his cot, Joey dreamed of Pato Rodríguez in the electric chair, hands free from their straps, cupped over his ears. When the lights dimmed, Pato called out, "Cinnamon." Joey woke, stared into the dark. He was sure of two things, that he hated Korea and that *his* death was out there, patient, walking in regulation boots.

Owens told Joey to just sleep. Master Sergeant Anderson had left camp without leaving orders for him. "Sleep," Owens said. "Enjoy the scenery."

Joey couldn't sleep because he was sure Anderson would be coming to take him to combat. "I hate Korea," he said.

"Got to stop the communists here or they'll be at your doorstep." Owens smiled.

Joey tried to imagine communists taking Michigan City. "I still hate it," he said.

"I hate being here," Owens said, looking from side to side, pulling on his belt buckle with his right hand. "I hate the fucking food the most."

"I hate it all."

"All of it?" Owens asked.

"All of it."

"The clothes, you hate the clothes?" He looked at Joey disbelievingly.

"I hate this uniform."

"I like the clothes." Owens smiled, looked down at his khaki T-shirt, jacket, pants. "They let you keep the clothes. And the tags." He held his dog tags to his face, read his name, looked again at Joey. "I bet you a jimmy you can't guess my blood type."

Joey thought the clothes didn't look bad on Owens, even though his T-shirt was inside out. "Bet a what?"

"A jimmy, you know, a favor," Owens said. "You win, I owe you. I win, you owe me."

"Type A," Joey said.

"It's O. Now you owe me one, Malone." Still smiling, he began to walk off.

"Owens, your shirt is inside out."

Owens stopped, looked at his shirt. "How can you tell?"

"Look at the collar."

He stretched the neck of his T-shirt out to look at it. "I think you're right." He looked back at Joey. "We're even."

Joey thought of Indiana like an alcoholic thinks of liquor. When he closed his eyes, he saw pictures: his backyard in Michigan City, the pitcher of lemonade his mother sets on the round table in the corner of the back porch, his mother in a yellow cotton dress, arms folded, smiling. He's playing catch with his father while his brother, only six, sits in the grass, rocking and watching. His father is teaching him to throw a curve, saying he is old enough now, his arm can withstand the violent snap of the wrist at the point of release. It's a warm day. The sun shines directly on his arms and face.

In Korea, the afternoon turned to a cutting cold. Sergeant Anderson had told Joey that winter in Korea was brutal. "Ever seen a man turn blue?" he'd said. Joey tried to block it out by thinking of Indiana, the smile that crosses his father's face as a pitch breaks a few inches. He couldn't make it last. Something always returned him to Korea: the smell of a rifle recently oiled, phosphorous clouds rising on the horizon. He wanted to stay back there with his mother still alive, his brother too young to know he can't learn how to read, his father squatting in freshly mowed grass, pointing two fingers toward a dish they'd taken to use as home plate. He knew that the dream wasn't real, that it never had been. But his mind went there, and for a moment the khaki uniform became jeans and a white T-shirt, the flapping of the flag became striped sheets on the clothesline, the birds lining the top of the tent became cardinals perched on a telephone wire, and even the leaves, as they turned, turned toward home.

Late afternoon with no sign of Sergeant Anderson, Joey and Owens played cards in the cab of a truck with a burnt-out transmission. They played poker, but Joey had too much trouble keeping track of the cards, so they played Go Fish, talked about California, Indiana, food, women. Owens said the problem with Korean whores was that, basically, they were white. "White women don't fuck worth a shit," he said. "Good to look at but no good on their backs." After another hand of Go Fish, he retracted the statement. "Truth is, this guy in basic told me that about white women. I never really had much luck with women, really." A jeep rattled by. Owens watched as if it meant something. "Truth is, I never had *any* luck with women." He turned back to Joey, put the deck of cards on the dash. "Look at this." He pulled out his wallet, opened it, removed a photograph, and held it up to Joey's face. The photograph was of a beautiful white girl with long dark hair parted down the middle.

"Who is she?" Joey asked.

"Her name is Barbara. I met her in geography."

"You go out with her?"

"You kidding? She gave me her picture when she found out I was going in the army." He turned the photograph to look at her again. "I hardly know her really. I seen her at school and stuff, but I don't know her mother or nothing. You think I'm stupid carrying her picture?"

"You mean everyone goes to the same school out there?"

"Yeah. Ain't no girls in your school?"

"Plenty of girls. No Negroes."

"Yeah. So this guy in basic told me carrying pictures of white women would either get me crazy or get me killed." Owens put the picture in his wallet, shuffled the cards. "He said I got the sickness of screwing black girls and pretending they're white."

Joey thought of himself with the whore, thinking of June.

"He's crazy," Owens said. "I never even been to bed with a woman, and he's telling me what I'm thinking." He began dealing the cards.

"Forget it," Joey said.

"What I'm worried about is getting shot up or killed, and I never do sleep with a girl. We *could* get killed here. There should be a rule."

"For the army or for the enemy?"

Owens laughed. "You think the communists would co-operate?"

"You think the army would?"

Owens took the picture back out of his wallet. He looked it over again carefully, then began tearing it into pieces. "If they ever do pass that rule, I don't want any doubt about me being eligible." He threw the pieces of photograph into the space between them in the cab. The pieces fluttered to the seat and floorboard like disembodied wings.

"We really could get killed," Owens said. "Especially *you*."

"You have a 7?" Joey said.

Owens shook his head. "Think that's why Anderson took you to Suzie's?"

"What do you mean?"

"You know, the rule."

Joey shrugged. "I slept with a girl just before I left Michigan City."

"Really? You got a queen?"

"Go fish," Joey said. He told Owens about June Norris, the night on the outfield grass. He told him about her pointing to the stars, pulling her dress over her head. They played another hand of Go Fish, and Owens asked Joey to tell it again. Afternoon faded into evening, night. They huddled in their jackets, kept the flashlight pointed toward the seat. Owens made Joey tell the story five times. He liked the idea of animals in the sky. At midnight, they stepped out of the truck to look for Little Bear. The sky was too full of clouds. They climbed back into the cab.

"You think I could meet her?" Owens said.

"I don't know where she is. You have a 5?"

"You just asked for a 5. You don't know what college she's gone to?"

"Somewhere in Arizona or New Mexico. You have a 6?"

"Fish," Owens said, shaking his head. "I been to Arizona once. Nothing special." He spread his cards, closed them. "She'll be coming home for summer, won't she? I don't want to hit on her. I just want to meet her."

"Okay."

"As soon as we get out of this shithole," Owens said.

"Yeah," Joey said, "as soon as we get out of here."

"You think your pop mind me staying with you?"

"You could fix his car," Joey said, laughing.

"What's he got?"

"A Pontiac. A big one."

"Probably a lot like a jeep."

"Doesn't look like a jeep. Looks more like a boat."

"I wouldn't tell your pop I want to meet June," Owens said. "He might get the wrong idea. Got a 9?"

"Go fish," Joey said.

Joey lay on his cot, unable to sleep, trying to figure out why his brother could not read. He thought it might be his fault. When Dave was really young, Joey used to sit with him and hold a picture book open, pretending to read, making up stories to go with the pictures. He wondered if his brother thought reading was some mystical thing having nothing to do with black letters on white sheets of paper. He remembered taking a head of lettuce, peeling off a leaf at a time, "reading" them to his brother. He'd promised to show Dave how to read stories on plankboard fences, cardboard boxes, photographs. The fogged window of a transport truck, Joey thought. He began crying silently.

He often cried in his cot. One night he'd cried because Pato Rodríguez stood with hands cupped over his ears as words he couldn't understand flew at him. One night he cried because they were building a bridge over Water Street years too late. One night he cried because he was worried about crying so much.

He was crying when Sergeant Anderson walked into the tent, squatted beside his cot. The gray stubble on Anderson's cheeks made him look ghostly. Joey tried to stop crying, couldn't. Sergeant Anderson said nothing, waited, finally spoke, "When I heard Paul, that's my brother. When I heard he was dead, I cried. Bawled like you wouldn't believe. North Africa's an awful place. Not as bad as here, but awful." He rubbed his nose with his thumb and forefinger. "MacArthur probably spends half his time crying. Ought to, anyway." Sergeant Anderson waited again, but Joey still couldn't stop crying. "Tomorrow'll be better. Going to join a combat unit. The both of us. No more lolling around here."

He stood, then squatted again close to Joey, whispered. "Once, for a while, I heard this voice. Didn't tell me to do things, that was the frustration of it. I could hear it but couldn't make it out. I'd think, it's the wind, or it's my lungs, or those noises that go on in the back of your skull. But it was a real voice and one night I finally made it out. It was asking questions."

Anderson whispered so close that his stubble brushed against Joey's cheek. Joey stopped crying.

"It asked, 'How is it?' and 'What of it?' and 'What are you waiting for?'" Anderson paused for a long time, then put his hand on Joey's shoulder. "We're soldiers. Tomorrow'll be like old times."

"What old times?" Joey said.

"I'll take care of you. Way my brother took care of me."

As soon as Anderson left, Joey cursed him, angry to have been caught crying over his brother. He wanted part of his life kept separate from Korea.

During the first day of the fight for Hill 409, Joey kept low in a bunker, shot his rifle at a large-leaved tree in the distance. The drive from the support unit to the front had taken less than an hour. In minutes he was in the bunker. The hill was a long, gradual incline, wooded near the top. Some strategy was being played out, Joey was sure, but all he could make of it was that the North Koreans controlled the hill, firing from behind the trees and foliage, and the army wanted it. Joey thought of several alternatives to fighting over the hill—a trade could be worked out, graders could level the thing, citizens of Michigan City could pitch in and buy it.

Joey was ankle-deep in icy mud. When the call came to withdraw, his feet were as heavy and awkward as bowling balls. He tried to run, slipped, fell, the icy ground hard as concrete. He flattened himself against it, crawled. Beside him a man yelled, "Jesus, my father," stood straight up, hands at his face as if he'd remembered something important. Mud covered his right shoulder and arm, his helmet tipped slightly to the left, his startled eyes the color of wet grass. Joey knew the standing man would draw attention. He rolled left, began running clumsily. He heard a burst of fire behind him and a sound like a baseball landing in a mitt. He didn't look.

That night, huddled around a small fire with a dozen other men, Joey tried to imagine pistons moving up and down like the legs of chorus girls. He thought about the Green Foxes' first baseman calling out "cinnamon" as he died, as if he were trying to tell Joey something, to let him know what to expect. Joey had no idea what to expect.

Sergeant Anderson squatted next to him, put his arm on Joey's shoulder. "We'll take that hill tomorrow," Anderson said.

Let them have it, Joey thought. There were thousands like it in Korea that had no North Koreans at the top.

Before the night was over, it had begun to snow.

During the second day of the fight for Hill 409, Joey muddled forward slowly across the snow-covered ground. He was frightened, crawling on his elbows and knees. Snow soaked through his clothing, and he lost some of his fear in the cold. The crawling forced water into his boots. His feet grew numb. From behind, the firing stepped up to provide more cover. Joey believed he would die that way, from friendly fire, although the yellow flashes kept coming from behind the trees at the top of the hill as well. Suddenly the ground in front of Joey erupted. He flattened, unmoving, terrified. His right foot felt warmer. It took him a few seconds to realize he had been wounded. The boot was filling with blood.

"Malone!" someone yelled. Joey had to resist the urge to stand. "Malone!" To his left. A man motioning. A ditch. Three other men. "Malone!" The air filled with sparks. "Malone!" Joey started crawling, keeping his head low. His feet didn't respond. "Malone!" He began rolling toward the ditch. The sound of mortar rose and fell like a scream heard through a revolving door. Suddenly he began flying toward the ditch. The impact of the explosion swallowed its initial sound, but the reverberations clanged in his skull. Hands pulled at his arms. Beneath the echo of the bell he heard a voice. "You ain't even hurt, bud." The blue of the sky rushed out east and west, leaving an enormous white.

A pair of feet, Joey saw them in the tangle of legs at the end of the ditch, thought they were his. He tried to move them, but the thick boots whiskered with frost would not budge. He brought his right hand to his mouth, covered his fist with a cloud of warmth. He believed he was ready to die. The night was silent, dark, lit only by a quarter moon. He hoped his death would be like Pato's, that the moon would dim momentarily, then, with a surge of light, become full. Joey felt his eyes draw closed. "Cinnamon," he said, laughing. The quarter moon became dim, distant. He closed his eyes, opened them. The urge to close them became more insistent. He opened them one last time, saw the full face of the moon near enough to touch. As his eyes closed, he heard a voice say, "I've found you."

The woman in the silent shoes with a dozen dog tags hanging from her wrist passed through the space between the beds. The man in the next bed tapped the floor so Joey would look at him. "I had the best treeing dog in Ballard County," he said.

Joey nodded.

The man pointed to his head. "The doctors here keep their heads in their hats, putting them on in the morning, taking them off before bed. They don't know what it is to be human."

"I had a dream," Joey said, "where the nurse had fingers strung around her neck."

"It wouldn't be so bad," the man said, "but I hate to leave before catching my limit."

They lay still. Joey listened to their breathing, believed the words had some value. He turned again, but the man had fallen asleep. Joey wanted to ask about his feet. Although everyone could see he had lost his feet, Joey couldn't help telling people. He wondered where they were. He thought the doctors might keep them floating in a large jar.

The doctors told Joey he was disoriented.

Dr. Perkins loved Joey's stumps, said he couldn't have had better care, that he was a showcase of army surgical skill. When Joey asked what he'd done with his feet, the doctor's face turned gray and he wouldn't say. He assured Joey that they were not in a laboratory jar. "The army does not keep feet," he said.

Joey stared at the end of the bed where his feet should be. He tried to spread his toes and could feel the muscles in the balls of his feet tighten, relax, threaten to cramp. "Phantom feelings," the doctor had said. Joey didn't believe him. Somewhere, floating in formaldehyde, his feet were dancing, he was sure.

Sergeant Anderson sat next to the bed in dress uniform, his back erect, his jaw set. He and Joey stared not quite at each other, one waiting for the other to begin.

"Proud of you," Anderson said.

"I lost my feet," Joey said.

Sergeant Anderson grimaced, tensed his neck. Joey thought he was holding something back as if angry. "I know, Malone. I know that." He looked over Joey's head at the wall.

They sat for several moments in silence. Joey felt he should say something. It dawned on him that he was going home and Sergeant Anderson couldn't control him now. Joey said nothing. Anderson's face was rigid, red, the muscles around his cheekbones thick and tense. Joey believed Anderson was about to burst into anger, say he should be proud to give his feet for his country. Joey looked away. It didn't matter, he thought.

When Joey looked back, tears were running down Anderson's face. "I searched for you. After the firing died down. If I'd gone another hundred yards, I'd found you. Finally did, of course." Sergeant Anderson cleared his throat, removed his handkerchief, wiped his face.

Joey again felt that he should say something. He had nothing to offer. Finally he asked, "What do you think they've done with them?"

"With what?" Anderson removed his dress hat, held it in his lap.

"My feet."

Anderson stared at Joey several moments, then crossed his legs. "Had to identify my brother by his hands. Most the rest of him was gone, just gone. I kept thinking, *This is Paul, this is Paul.*" Sergeant Anderson put his dress hat back on, uncrossed his legs, then took his hat off again. "My brother had big hands, like a boxer's." He made two fists, held them at his chest. "What they showed me were two little cauliflowers."

"I can feel my feet," Joey said. "I can wiggle my toes."

"Everybody gets things taken away from them." Anderson stood. "Got to make do with what's left." He shook hands with Joey for a long time, then left him.

Owens came late, had to wake Joey to talk. It was after visiting hours, but the nurse made an exception.

"You all right?" Owens said.

Joey opened his eyes, looked at Owens running his hands up and down his arms.

"You all right, man? It's colder than Bejesus out there."

"I lost my feet," Joey said.

"That's what I heard. I'm sorry, Joey." Owens took off his green wool pullover cap, dusted with frost. "I got a deck with me if you feel up to it." He sat on the edge of the bed.

Joey raised himself up on one elbow. "What do you think they did with them?"

Owens shuffled the cards once, then looked at Joey. "They probably got a whole warehouse full of them."

Joey nodded. They played Go Fish. "Anderson worked it out that I could come," Owens said. "He told me, 'You can remake a human soul just like you can rebuild an engine.' What do you think of that? I don't think he's running with all his cylinders."

"You have a 4?"

"You just asked for a 4. He told me they took that hill the next day."

"So the communists are that much farther from Michigan City?"

Owens smiled. "Something like that." They played Go Fish again and again. Owens asked about the Negro in the next bed. Joey told him he'd seen the man crying during the night, his left arm, just a stub, twitching around like a propeller.

Owens shook his head, dealt another hand. "Tell me again. About June and Little Bear."

"It was the end of the school year," Joey said and told about the baseball field, June pointing, how she pulled her dress over her head.

When he finished, Owens walked over to the window. "Damn, Joey, more stars than you can imagine tonight. I know Little Bear is out there, if I knew where to look."

"Let me see," Joey said.

"How am I going to do that?" Owens said. They stared at each other for a moment before Owens began crying. "This fucking shithole," he said. He walked to the bed, slipped his

DANCING IN THE MOVIES

arms under Joey's back and knees. "Be quiet," he said. He lifted Joey out of the bed.

Joey heard the nurse calling after them in a hushed voice. Owens carried him to the door and out into the night. The cold air wrapped around Joey's throat like a hand. The stub ends of his legs ached. He could no longer feel his lost feet.

Joey looked over the sky, blurred his eyes until he could make out the round buttocks and chubby head of a bear cub. He lifted his right arm into the air, pointed to the sky. "Ursa Minor," he said.

"Little Bear," Owens said.

They stared into a sky blistered with stars.

Kentucky

Once when I was eleven years old, my father asked me not to buy him cigarettes, even if he begged me to. We had just moved back to Kentucky and were staying with Aunt Hannah, Mother's big sister, while Dad tried to find work. The white clapboard house had two bedrooms, but the room that had been Grandfather's was not used and the door was locked. The house overlooked Highway 60 from a steep but short hill. Across the highway, set close to the road, was Hale's Cafe, a rectangular building with huge windows on either side of the front door and an immense gravel parking lot flanking it. A pole near the two-lane highway held a neon sign high above the building. HALE'S was written in cursive red neon, CAFE in thin yellow neon, and around them both was a glowing blue oval. For my brother Ask and me, the cafe was the only source of entertainment.

During the day we went over to Hale's six or seven times to buy sodas, play the jukebox, or push nickels through the pinball machine. Jennetta worked there. She knew our father and let me buy cigarettes because she knew they were for him. When Dad took me aside that Friday night and asked me not to buy him cigarettes, he meant he didn't want me to go to Hale's the next day and stick a quarter in the cigarette machine for Kent regulars. He had decided to quit smoking.

It had been a summer for decisions. Just a few weeks earlier, he had decided to return to Kentucky from Arizona. He said he needed folks he could *talk* to. He was making a new start in an old place, and I guess that made him think it would be a good time to quit smoking. He hadn't liked Arizona. We'd lived in a small town on the Gila River and he'd taught eighth graders about the American system of government. Something had dissatisfied him—the administration, he said once; the desert, dry as asphalt; the puny trickle of water they called a river. Mother told me it was something else, something we were too young to understand. Whatever the reason, he announced one day that we were leaving, and not long afterward we left.

Charley was the only one mad about it. He was just a year away from graduating from high school and wanted to finish with the kids he knew in Arizona. Ask and I had friends too, but no one took the friendships of nine- and eleven-year-olds too seriously. Mother's people were still in Kentucky, so she was willing though not eager to come back. Cassie was only five and happy wherever she was, although she was the reason we'd moved to Arizona in the first place. The doctors said she needed drier air, so we'd headed west for two and a half years. Since her breathing problems had cleared up, my father assumed we could return.

Charley was the loudest complainer. He was our brother for certain, but you couldn't tell from looking. Ask and I were sometimes mistaken for twins, even though I was two years older. We both had high foreheads, light skin, and domed skulls. I was so skinny my head looked like a watermelon on my neck, but because of its shape, kids in the first grade had labeled me Peanut Head. My major concern about returning to Kentucky was that someone would dredge that name up again. People in Arizona had just called me Tom and I'd been happy with that. Ask's head was normal and he was heavier, but we still looked alike. Charley, on the other hand, was real handsome, like Sal Mineo without the sneer.

Supper was at six at Aunt Hannah's always. At our real house, supper had been whenever it was ready, but Aunt Hannah liked things to have order. She used to say, "The top should be on the top." So we ate at six. Any trips to Hale's had to be before then. We weren't allowed to cross the highway after supper; Father said he didn't like the crowd that gathered there after dark. The night he asked me not to buy him cigarettes, we had made one last run at 5:45. The neon sign was already on and Elvis was singing "Jailhouse Rock." A big boy, nearly grown, with a package of Kools rolled up in the arm of his T-shirt, had the bases loaded on the pinball machine. Jennetta leaned over the counter and smiled at us.

"How's my little men?" she said. "Cokes?"

I nodded and we climbed up on the stools. They were perfectly round, supported by one chrome leg, and could spin either way without stopping. Ask had taped a penny on the edge once and I had spun while he counted over a hundred revolutions before my arm got tired and I quit. Hale's had nine booths with red vinyl seats and green tables trimmed with polished aluminum. Each booth had a miniature jukebox with the songs listed on cards like a menu. Every Elvis single I could remember was there, plus Chubby Checker singing "The Twist." But *every* jukebox had them; what Hale's also had was Chuck Berry, Jerry Lee Lewis, and even Little Richard. At night it was loud. Ask and I could hear it clear up the hill, across the highway.

Jennetta brought us our Cokes. She had the blackest hair imaginable, black like paint, and blue eyes, the kind of blue the sky gets at night. I couldn't say she was beautiful, but with her hair tied back in a blue handkerchief and just a few strands teasing across her forehead, I understood even then that something about her was magical. I could see it with my own eyes. Ask couldn't. He liked blondes like Marilyn Monroe. He *knew* she was pretty, everybody said so. But to me, Jennetta had the same something Marilyn had, whatever that was. She was a few years younger than Mother, which made her thirty-three or thirty-four.

We had to hurry to get back before six. After supper we lay on the grass overlooking Hale's and talked about the differences between Arizona and Kentucky. What we missed most were the lizards. My favorites were the striped ones you could chase for an hour, and if you caught one by the tail, it'd snap off and squiggle around in your hand. Over the next couple of weeks you'd see a bare-butt lizard hustling around until its tail grew back. Ask liked horny toads. They depended on camouflage for protection, but once you spotted them, they were easy to catch. He'd tried keeping one in a shoebox, but it died, which led to a lecture from Mother about the wild being wild. That night I told Ask the difference between him and me was the way we liked to catch lizards.

We counted cars on the highway. I had the northbound and he had the south. With him leading 36 to 18, I conceded, secretly happy I was behind, because he would never have given in and I'd have had to look into my hands or stare at the moon whenever I heard a northbound vehicle until we were tied. Ask never conceded anything. That was probably why Dad always asked me to buy him cigarettes. Ask wouldn't do it. He didn't like smoke. Of course, Dad could have bought the cigarettes himself, but he avoided the cafe.

Back inside, we listened to the Cardinals game. They had just traded for a new left fielder who was supposed to bring some power into the lineup, but he had come from the Cubs. We weren't too hopeful. Charley had gone to a Sally League baseball game with Limber Watkins, and I could tell our parents were relieved that he was becoming reacquainted with old friends, so he might be less hostile. About the fifth inning, the Cards trailed the Phillies by seven and we gave up on them. Mother suggested that Ask and I get ready for bed. It was then my father made his request.

My father was tall and thin, with dark red hair and blue eyes. He had a serious face, but he liked to laugh and I liked to listen to it. We all did. His laughter made me laugh, a good thing for a laugh to do. He came to me with his hands in his pockets, wearing his green hunting shirt, tan slacks, and the brown wingtips he'd had for years. He was forty-three then, about the same age as several of the astronauts—a fact he often pointed out. "Tom," he started, gesturing for me to walk into the kitchen with him. "I don't want you to buy cigarettes for me tomorrow. Even if I ask you to do it."

I was a little puzzled, but I nodded.

"No matter how much I ask. Can you do that for me?"

I nodded again and that was the end of it.

In that tiny house made tinier by the locked-up room, Mother, Father, and Cassie slept in the bed in Aunt Hannah's room, leaving her to sleep on the couch. We boys slept on the front porch. Ask and I got into our pajamas and crawled into the makeshift bed—two quilts beneath us and a sheet on top. Since Aunt Hannah went to bed early on the couch, our parents had to do the same. By 10:15 we were able to sneak out to the edge of the hill and watch Hale's.

Already a pretty good crowd milled about the checkered floor. Others ate burgers or barbecue in the booths. One couple danced near the back, and a crowd watched someone rack up points on the pinball. The parking lot filled with station wagons borrowed from worried parents, pickups, a couple of bugs, and always two or three hot rods with chrome pipes and grills, their bodies painted candy apple red or metallic sparkle blue. Boys gathered around the side of the building to drink beer bought in Illinois (our county was dry) and tell stories so loud that we could catch parts about racing their cars, beating up their friends, or feeling up their girls. If there was nothing real to talk about, they'd dream about Jennetta.

After working most of the day behind the counter, Jennetta waited tables at night. She was the star of Hale's Cafe. Even Ask admitted he couldn't keep from looking at her, especially when one of her favorite songs came on the jukebox and she pulled some lucky boy up from his seat to dance. She liked Little Richard, who was my favorite—Ask preferred Elvis, who he *knew* was good.

Then Charley arrived. He and Limber Watkins must have pulled in while we were watching Jennetta, because suddenly there he was posing in the doorway, the collar of his shirt turned up, sleeves rolled to his elbows. Jennetta clapped her hands when she saw him and gave him a big hug.

"Did you see that?" Ask said.

"She hugged him," I said. We watched our brother walk

like the other boys we'd seen, swiveling his hips a little, leading with his chest. He sat in a booth facing us, next to a girl with a ponytail. She was cute enough, but after Jennetta hugged you, how could you be interested in anyone else?

We watched for almost an hour until we were both about to fall asleep. Just as Ask suggested we go back to the porch, Charley walked out of Hale's, stopping at the door to wave and say something. He had taken only a couple of steps in the parking lot before Jennetta came hurrying after him. She took his arm and leaned up close like she was whispering. They paused for a moment, and we paused with them, not even breathing. Ask and I both leaned closer, although we had no chance of hearing. They began walking around the corner of the building on our blind side. We had to run across the yard to see them—dangerous because this put us in front of our parents' bedroom window, but a risk we were willing to take.

Jennetta leaned against the white wall, but only her shoulders touched Hale's. Her body slanted away from the building toward Charley. He put his hand on the wall next to her head and leaned on that arm. One of her hands, on his chest, fooled with his shirt or his buttons or something we couldn't quite see. He bent slowly forward, closer to her. We knew at any moment it could happen—our brother was going to kiss Jennetta *on the lips*. Somebody put "Love Me Tender" on the jukebox and they both laughed.

Then something funny happened. Even though she still fiddled with his shirt, his head started creeping back until he stood straight, no weight on the hand against the wall. He pulled his hand away and shoved it in his pocket. Jennetta took his arm at the elbow, but he shook his head and walked away from her. At the neon sign he stopped and turned back. Ask and I expected something like in the movies where the man gives in, says he loves her, and they rush into each other's arms. That didn't happen. We heard what my brother called out to Jennetta. He said, "Fuck you."

Charley came straight across the street. We had to run back to the porch, jerk the sheet up around us, and pretend to sleep. He must have flown up the hill, because we had barely shut our eyes before he was there, sitting on the steps, staring out at the cafe. We lay silent as bricks, barely breathing—the way people pretend to sleep is almost always to pretend to be dead. We were so quiet that when Charley muttered under his breath it sounded like it had come over a loudspeaker. "Hicks," he said and lay back against the floor.

I couldn't take it any more and looked at him with my best sleepy face. His feet were on the top step, back flat against the porch, hands behind his head, knees wide apart forming a diamond. "That you, Charley?" I kept one eye only half opened.

"Go back to sleep," he said.

Ask jumped at that. "What's going on?" he said, scratching his head as he raised up. I gave him a mean look for overacting, but he just scrunched up his face at me.

"Go back to sleep," Charley said again.

"Good ball game?" I asked.

He didn't say anything.

Ask sat up straight. "What's wrong, Charley?"

"Nothing's wrong with me. Why aren't you guys asleep?"

"You woke us up," I said.

"I didn't wake anybody up." He finally turned and looked at us, propping himself on one elbow. "Stay up late listening to the Cards?"

I nodded. "Phillies beat them."

"I hate baseball," he said. "I just wanted out of the house."

Ask and I looked at each other, then Ask said, "Where'd you go?"

Charley shrugged and looked at the floor. "Places. A bar, maybe. What would you think of that?"

"How could you get into a bar?" I asked.

"Some people think I look pretty mature. Some people think I'm full grown. You going to run to Mom with this?"

"Heck no," I said. Ask was too offended to reply.

"We went to Cairo in Limber's Chevy. He's got it souped up and cherried out. I ought to have a car like that." He looked back at the cafe. "Everybody ought to."

"You went to a bar." Ask didn't want the story to fizzle out.

"Kind of. We got this guy to go into a bar and buy us a six of Budweiser. Me and Limber drank all of them. But there's nowhere to go in this hick town."

I waited to see if he was going to offer more. "There's Hale's," I said finally. Charley narrowed his eyes at me. "Me and Ask like going there," I added. Charley relaxed but Ask seemed tense, so I elbowed him under the sheet.

"We went there too. After the beer." He sat up and looked at the cafe. I hooked my head around the porch railing, but all I could see was neon red, yellow, blue.

Nobody said anything for a long while, and I thought we might wind up going to sleep without knowing. I expected Ask to be close to gone since he could never stay awake for anything, even Jerry Lewis movies, but he was wide awake, staring at our brother. Charley finally broke the silence. "Wouldn't be a bad place except for that woman."

My heart started to beat like I was scared. "I like Jennetta," I said. He didn't seem to hear me. "I think she's all right."

"You're too young to understand," he said.

Ask had this look on his face, like his eyes had turned into marbles, a look he got whenever he was trying to fight off doing something he knew he shouldn't do. This time I was sure exactly what it was. He was close to asking Charley outright. I poked him with my elbow to snap him out of it. He didn't even turn his head. I hit him again, a mistake, because the words just popped out of his mouth. "We were watching," he said. "We saw you and Jennetta from the hill. We heard you too."

"Heard what?"

"What you said to her," I said.

Charley didn't do anything but stare at us, then back at the cafe.

"What happened?" Ask said.

"You're not old enough to understand," he said.

"Fuck you," Ask said. Charley and I snapped our heads around to look at him. His eyes weren't marbles anymore. I don't know if Charley realized when I did, but he must have soon afterward, that Ask wouldn't quit until he got an answer, even if it meant talking to Jennetta. That's just the way he was, even hitting him wouldn't change anything once he got it in his head to do something.

Charley lay back again and scooted closer to us. "She wanted me to give a message to Dad. She said I was mature enough to understand." He moved even closer, until I could feel his breath when he whispered, as if the words themselves were pushing against my face. "She said I should tell him she'd wait for him to work things out."

It was a funny thing then. I started crying. Ask didn't, neither did Charley, just me, my face in the blankets, Charley going "shh," and Ask running his hand through my hair the way Mother always did. I didn't cry long and lifted my head to wipe my eyes and nose.

"What was that all about?" Charley said.

"I don't know," I said. "I couldn't help it."

"Maybe she can't help it either," Ask said. I could tell from the way he said it that he was trying to make me feel better.

The next day Ask and I went to Hale's and Jennetta was there by herself, frying eggs for her breakfast behind the counter. "Too early for Cokes," she said, smiling at us, then looking back at the eggs. "Your daddy'd skin you alive, drinking Coca-Cola this early."

It should have been the same. Her voice floated like it always did, she talked with us like we were real people, but we both knew it was spoiled. Even though we'd come not for sodas but to play pinball, we turned around and left.

Just before noon, Father stepped out onto the porch and called me. Ask and I had been playing baseball according to who picked the snazziest car to come next on the highway. He was ahead 6 to 3. I walked up the porch steps and Father offered me a quarter and two dimes. "Pick me up some Kents. You and Ask get yourselves Cokes."

I shook my head. "You told me not to."

"I'm telling you to do it now."

"Last night . . ."

"Forget what I said last night. I changed my mind." He slipped the coins in my shirt pocket, patted me on the shoulder, and gave me a lopsided nod. "Come on, partner."

By this time Ask had walked up behind me. He stared at us all marble-eyed, which scared me. I must have been shaking my head no, because Father said, "Am I going to have to go across and get them? You boys run over there all day."

Ask climbed the porch steps beside me. "I'll get them," he said.

The two of us walked down the hill and across the highway to Hale's together. Jennetta called out to us as we entered, but neither of us paid any attention. We walked straight to the cigarette machine. I gave Ask the quarter. He slipped it into the slot and pulled the knob. When the package fell into the tray, he pulled out the tail of his shirt and picked it up with his shirttail between the package and his hand. Jennetta stared funny at us walking out. Ask held the cigarettes away from his body and had to walk limp-legged, his face screwed up like he'd been eating lemons. I helped him up the hill and waited on the porch while he walked in the house and dropped the Kents on the couch next to our father.

We didn't stay in Kentucky too long. Cassie started choking on the air again, and by the end of the summer we were in another little town in Arizona. Our father never stopped smoking; whatever it was in Kentucky he'd returned to look for, he never found in Arizona. I don't know what it was, although I'm pretty sure it wasn't just Jennetta. The last time I asked my mother, she shrugged her shoulders. "Sometimes people want to be happier than anyone has a right to be," she said.

And once while I was in high school and Charley was going through a tough divorce, he told me to hide his gun and not give it to him no matter how hard he asked. He dropped it on my bed, a big revolver. I took a towel from the bathroom after he left and wrapped the gun. Then I rode my ten-speed to the junior high where Ask went, arriving just as he was getting on the bus to go home. We rode to a park. I showed him the gun. We made a plan.

We biked past the edge of town, beyond the citrus groves, to the county dump. Ask picked a spot full of rotting vegetables and crushed glass. We dropped the gun there, then dragged a stained mattress over it. With him on the seat and me standing, pumping the pedals, we rode all the way downtown. I called Mother and told her we were going to the movies. Normally she would have been angry with us for missing supper, but she seemed happy to have us out of the way. We saw *Barbarella* twice, then rode home in the dark.

The light in my room was on. The sheets and blankets had been ripped off the mattress. The mattress was turned sideways on the box spring. All the drawers in the dresser were pulled out, with shirt sleeves and socks hanging over the lips. On the floor, in the center of the room, Charley lay asleep. Ask threw a blanket over him and I turned off the light.

It was a tight squeeze, the both of us in Ask's bed, and I couldn't help but think about Aunt Hannah's porch. I asked if he remembered. "Of course I do," he said, offended that I had to ask.

Dancing in the Movies

"Bob Marley dead," Eugene said, hand at his dick as he walked in the door, brown face yellowed from heroin, eyes puffy like a boxer's. He stared hard at me, leaned against a barstool. His shoulders made a big spread, but he was junk skinny, that all-sucked-out look. "Bob Marley *dead*," he said again, like I couldn't hear.

I wanted to call him a lemon-faced nigger, but I didn't like that ugly side and kept it quiet, even with Eugene. I got straight to the point. "You seen Dee?"

"Didn't you hear me?" He gripped at the air, making two large fists, his voice full of anger and familiarity, as if I hadn't been gone for months.

"I already heard," I said. My best friend, Lonnie, had picked me up at the bus station and given me the news. "It's all over the radio," he said. "The industrialists killed him." I felt weak, twenty hours on a Greyhound, then I hear Marley is gone. I asked Lonnie how they killed him. "Cancer," he said, "white man's disease." It had sounded like an accusation.

"Shit," Eugene said, bending close to study my face for signs of anguish. He crossed his arms to make himself bigger. "Go listen at your fucking Elton John."

I felt accused again, as if my white skin had contributed to Marley's death. I would not apologize for being white, especially not to a bone-hollow junkie like Eugene. I stood and threw what was left of my beer in his face. "Where's Dee?"

For a moment his eyes sparked, but they clouded quickly. He seemed to shrink. "Shit, Freddie, why you always got a hard-on?" He wiped at his face, eyebrows. Beer ran down his fingers and dripped onto the concrete floor. "I don't know where she is. We ain't in no club."

"I need to find her." I sat again on the wood ladder-back chair, already regretting throwing the beer. "I need to find her, Eugene."

He turned away from me, wiping the last of the beer on his jeans, and walked to the jukebox. "Ask Wilson," he said.

Wilson was Lonnie's little brother. "Wilson's clean," I said. With Lonnie's help, Wilson had put down heroin and begun avoiding junkies, which meant he would have nothing to do with Dee. "Wilson is clean," I said again, louder.

Eugene paid no attention, slipping coins into the machine. As kids, Eugene and I had been friends, part of the neighborhood crowd that centered around Lonnie. Dee had been the only girl in the group and my girlfriend, off and on, since fourth grade. It was hard for me to remember a time I didn't love Dee. We cheated together on spelling, stole cigarettes from Quick Mart, made a wreath from oleander leaves for her mother's grave.

I knew where to find Wilson, although I didn't think he'd know where to find Dee. From noon to five Wilson sat in front of the Unemployment office, hoping to find *his* girlfriend. She left him because he couldn't quit heroin. Now he was clean, but she was gone.

Eugene bent over the jukebox, ran his index finger down the song list. He looked like a Norman Rockwell parody, big and childish, black and gaunt. He reminded me of a letter from Lonnie. *I used to think junkies were like little kids*, he wrote. *They're more like dead people playing human.* I decided to look for Wilson. He, at least, would be sympathetic—we were both looking for girlfriends.

I walked out of the Bree Lounge. The rain had stopped but the sky was still hooded with clouds. Music started up inside the bar, too muffled to be recognizable. I thought it must be Bob Marley. Dee and I had seen Bob Marley once in LA, so stoned we had to dance in our chairs. Lonnie had been with us, doing spins and dancing funk to reggae. Some song made us cry, just the sound of it, the way it moved inside. Lonnie enjoyed crying, but Dee and I weren't criers. It was Marley himself, singing with his whole body, moving like a marionette, then a dancer, that made the music into something liquid. I pictured Marley, bare to his waist, the blue light shining off his sweaty back, his dark hands on the silver microphone stand, but all I could hear was the muffled music from the Bree. I headed for the Unemployment building.

Downtown was noisy as a bad movie. Vested men carrying briefcases hurried past. They looked straight ahead, their thin, high-polish shoes finding the dry spots of the sidewalks. I almost fit in, wearing my best blue slacks and olive shirt, wanting to look good when I found Dee. In her last letter, she had written, *All the streets in Langston run the wrong way—that's why we grew up lost.* In response, I sent her a bus ticket. I didn't hear from her after that. My letters were returned.

Wilson sat in Lonnie's cream Coupe de Ville, drinking Burgie from the can. He rolled down the window on the passenger side and yelled. "Get in before it rains some more." He put a cold Burgie in my hand. "I love the rain," he said, "but from the inside."

I nodded, drank a swallow of beer. Flower vendors were back on the corners. The thin green paper tore when they tried to pull it off the stems of the rain-flattened flowers. The women with the flowers reminded me of Dee. Why? Because they smiled and waved the bouquets like Dee finding the phone book under a pile of magazines? Because I bought her flowers once? Lonnie told me I have a blindness for Dee; whatever I did, I was thinking how she could fit in, even if I was with my parents, who hated her, or in a class hundreds of miles from her. Then I remembered the cemetery. We had bought flowers for the graves last December, the day before I left Langston. Dee took me to where her mother, grandmother, and aunt were buried. She started crying, not because those dead women were dead, but because they didn't have any better imagination than to keep planting themselves one next to another. She had told me she wanted to be buried where everyone was a stranger. It was then she promised to come to Oregon in the summer.

Wilson was wearing a long-sleeved T-shirt and jeans speckled with white paint. He worked from six to noon, then watched the Unemployment building. The flecks of paint in his hair made him look like an old man. "Any sign of Angela?" I asked.

"It's tough," Wilson said. "Paper says unemployment is up though. I'm optimistic."

I could tell from his eyes he was still clean, although I didn't know him as a first-rate friend but through his brother Lonnie. I knew heroin enough to know clean, even though Dee told me that was bullshit. She said I didn't know heroin because I was straight, that I didn't know women because I was male, that I didn't know black because I was white. I just threw it back at her upside down to make her hush.

Wilson was two years younger than Lonnie and me, a junkie since he was thirteen. He used to stumble through our parties, giggling and scratching at himself. Lonnie had tried to get him to put down junk, but nothing had worked. When Wilson moved in with Angela, who was also a junkie, Lonnie bore down on her until she quit. But she couldn't endure Wilson's trying, especially when he'd get sick from shooting up again. It was her leaving that finally got him to quit. I had never felt close to Wilson before then, sharing the front seat of Lonnie's car, each of us looking for a woman who probably didn't want to be found. And something more—Wilson had been a junkie for years and quit. It gave me hope for Dee.

A Mexican woman with a sour-looking kid walked out of the Unemployment building. "You think of Welfare?" I asked. The first drop of rain hit center like a huge bug splat just below the rearview mirror.

"Starting again," Wilson said. He leaned forward, looked up to the dark sky. "Welfare's a waste of time. She's too proud. Too crazy. Too stupid."

I looked at the way his long neck curved as he stared at the sky. I pictured Angela walking by, seeing Wilson craning his head up and knowing instantly that he was clean. Thinking about it reminded me of my own problems. "You know where Dee is?"

Wilson gave a short laugh. "I can't find my own woman."

"Eugene said you might know."

"Fuck Eugene." Another drop hit right above his face. "They look like stars exploding," he said, then straightened. "Why don't you just get another woman?"

I shook my head, thinking that was what Eugene wanted to say in the bar, only he would have come out and said, "Why don't you get a *white* woman?" I didn't get angry with Wilson. We both had our ugly sides. "I love Dee," I said.

"Yeah," he said, looking at the Unemployment door as a man in a tie walked out. "They closing up. You need a ride somewhere?"

Wilson dropped me off at Lonnie's apartment, saying only that Dee got junk from Eugene. If I stayed close to Eugene, she would show.

Lonnie was smoking a joint. I didn't want any, even though he acted hurt and told me how wonderful it was with that effeminate twist in his voice. Everyone thought he was queer, but Lonnie was always after women and women were always after him.

"Maybe you should forget about Dee," Lonnie said, sitting with his legs crossed under him at one end of his record collection, flipping through the albums. He wore a smoke-colored shirt with a short collar and pleated beige pants, though he wasn't going anywhere and expecting no one but me.

"I love Dee." I squatted at the other end of the records. We looked for Bob Marley, moving crablike across the floor, checking each of the albums that lined the wall. Lonnie decided he must have lent the albums out. We settled for Peter Tosh, *Equal Rights.*

The five months I had been at college, Lonnie and Dee

were the only ones who had written. Lonnie's letters covered everything—from how well he was doing at work to how hard it was for his brother to quit junk. He had his own stationery—heavy blue paper with thick and thin black lines bordering it and a big *L.W.* at the top. Dee's letters came on whatever was handy while she was high and missing me. Once she had mailed a napkin from the Bree, scribbled up and blurred from wet-glass circles. Her letters were short, choppy, full of things that only half made sense. *I can't talk on telephones*, she wrote, *my throat swells up the size of testicles you seen in pictures—you love me or you just love niggers?* Her last letter said, *The birds are loose in Langston and all the streets run the wrong way, I eat drugs, Freddie.* When I had left, she'd just been fooling with heroin. With each letter she seemed more and more a junkie, until she started calling herself one. *Which your parents going to hate worser? Dee the nigger or Dee the junkie?*

"It's such a tacky love," Lonnie said. He sat, recrossed his legs, twisting his top foot behind a knee, like pretzels. "You need a cleaner love."

"I'm taking her back. I've got school housing and work study. I can afford it."

"Oh, Freddie, why on earth do you want to love Dee?" He leaned against the long fingers of his left hand, pushing his mouth into a half smile.

"Didn't say I want to. I just do."

"Huck Finn and Nigger Jim," Lonnie said.

"What's that supposed to mean?"

"It's a complex boys get where they feel they have to love what they hate." His head gave a little waggle as he said it.

"That'd explain why *you* chase after women," I said, happy for the chance to turn it upside down on him.

"You're such a clever boy," he said, flipping both hands open and spreading his fingers, then letting them fall limp at the wrists—his best fake fag gesture. "I suppose it would also explain why you hang out with me." He laughed, a giggle, and not fake. "Really, Dee and I are perfect for you: multiple outcasts."

He wanted me to laugh, forget about Dee for now, but I wouldn't buy it. "I've known you and Dee all my life."

"She smokes constantly. It's such a dirty habit." Suddenly he stood, twisting as he came out of the pretzel. "Wait here. Bob Marley may be in my closet."

"It's time someone came out of your closet," I said.

Lonnie couldn't find the album he wanted but returned with some old Temptations. "You remember?" he asked, flashing the album cover and doing a crossover step.

When we were kids we sang backup together on Temptations and Four Tops albums, complete with steps and hand moves. Lonnie had been the best in the neighborhood and he still loved to do it. I jumped up beside him. We rocked together to get in time. "Just My Imagination" was the song and it called for finger snapping at the hips, lots of hand movements to show nothing was real. The steps were just a little box with plenty of sway. We worked well together. All that was missing was Dee to sing the Eddie Kendricks high notes. Once I thought about that, I knew I would only dance through one song. Wherever I was, Dee was what was missing.

The Bree was quiet—a couple of the regular drunks at the bar, a heavy-thighed black woman we used to call Sisters because she was so fat, a dog-faced junkie who knew me and had breath like turpentine, a few others sipping beer or sleeping head down on the cheap tables. In the corner, an ugly red dog with a pointed nose chewed his leg. Nobody was saying where Eugene might be.

I was ready to leave when Dee walked in, hair knotted back on her head and body too thin, but still beautiful in jeans and a purple blouse, baggy so her ribs didn't show. She smiled when she saw me and came straight over. Dee carried heroin in her eyes. They became milky and thick, moved too slow.

Her arms went right around me, elbows at my ribs, hands

pressed against my shoulder blades. The kissing took me back to December, before I left, as if time were something people carried with them, the way some carried pictures.

"I've been looking for you," I said.

"Wilson told me." She ran her hands down then up my sides. "You look good," she said. "You got your Lonnie clothes on."

I laughed. I hadn't realized it, but everything I had on had been given to me at Christmases or birthdays by Lonnie.

"How's your college?" she said.

"I've got a place now. I want you to come back with me."

She smiled and sat at the table. "Get me a Coke."

I came back with a Coke and a beer. Dee sat, legs crossed, arms folded, leaning back and smiling, lipstick too red and smeared under her nose where she'd missed her lip.

"I mean it, Dee. This is a way out."

"Can't be." She took a big swallow of Coke.

"Why not?"

"If it was, we wouldn't know about it." Her upper lip glistened with Coke. She took another big drink, wiped her mouth with her hand. "Anyway, I don't like mixed marriages."

"Fuck that."

"They don't work, junkies and straights." She reached over and twisted one of my shirt buttons. "You'd have to take to junk."

I leaned back. The chair squeaked. Her milky eyes caught up with me. "I was thinking you could quit," I said.

Her hand moved up and down the glass. "You want to consume me." She wiped the cold sweat from the glass onto her forehead, the bridge of her nose, her eyelids.

"Wilson quit."

Her hand dropped to her lap. "That's what got you all excited, ain't it?"

"Lonnie got him through it."

She glared at me, only it was a fake look, like Lonnie's fake fag moves, meaning just the opposite. I tilted my head to show her I knew what she was doing. It must have reminded her of how long I had loved her because she went soft, showed her tongue as she smiled. Then she moved in another direction. Something came to her and her eyes flitted down to the table. "I'm one up on you," she said. "You go to college to figure out what it is *worth* getting up for." She looked up at me, thick eyes set hard against mine. "I got my reason to live."

She made me feel small, like junkies were the only full-grown people. "I tried the shit," I said, feeling stupid as soon as I said it because she knew I only snorted it. It was the needles I couldn't stand. I couldn't even look at them. But it was more than that. Junkies made me angry, especially gone junkies like Eugene, but even the clever ones, the pretty ones, the ones who could be anybody.

Dee's laugh was like a gurgle, but low enough to be a moan. "Snorting junk is like jacking off, a waste of good stuff."

I couldn't get mad at Dee. Every expression on her face was one I'd seen before, like old songs I never got tired of. "I love you, Dee."

"Love is the spike." Someone said this to her or she read it, because she just spat it out the way some people say "dig it," as if rehearsed. She couldn't even look at me, but I didn't know what to say or how to explain. I said what she already knew.

"I'm scared of needles."

"I'm scared of white college boys in short sleeves." She looked at me, started to look away, but I took her chin and turned her toward me.

"I want you to come with me."

"I want a Marlboro, all I've got are Kents." She lifted her purse from her lap. "Eugene smokes Kents."

"I got Luckies."

"Lucky Strikes are for lunatics."

"Then don't smoke." I leaned back. The chair squeaked again.

"I always smoke with heroin. It's what I do best. Or go with Eugene and get our shoes shined at Kresge's." She leaned way over the table, cupped *my* chin in her palm. "It's just like making love. That brush move through you like words move through your throat." She laughed, pulled me close, whispered as if it were a secret. "It's like dancing in the movies, when the music starts up and everyone knows their steps even though they're all strangers." She let go of my chin. "You try it. You *really* love me, then try it."

We sat without talking. I needed to convince her to leave goons like Eugene and the dog-faced black bastard at the next table, but I couldn't come up with the words. I knew what I didn't want to talk about—she was always wanting me to try the needle just once. Before she had become a junkie, when she was just using it now and then, she thought it would prove something. "You want to love me, you got to get a little dirty," she had said. I couldn't. I tried to change the subject. "Bob Marley died. Cancer."

She rocked her head without showing any emotion at all.

I needed the words to say how I had missed her, how other girls seemed plain and empty, how we could beat it if she'd just come with me. All that came in my head were the old clichés—*You have to believe in our love—we could make it if we believed in each other.* Dee hated those kinds of things, called them blind talking. I knew she wouldn't like it but said, "You have to have some faith."

Saying this, I reminded her of something, maybe something she'd heard, maybe just the way I could be, my limitations. Some little recognition flashed in and she came up with one of her Dee-isms. "Faith is the wooden pistol that gets you killed."

"What's that mean?"

She bit her lower lip, looked to the right, the left. "You try it once and I'll go with you."

My throat knotted. It came down to a trade. She'd try my

way if I'd try hers. She smiled at me, knowing I was too scared to do it. I decided to throw her fear back at her. "Clean?"

"Jesus, Freddie."

"You've got to quit. We can talk to Lonnie and Wilson."

"I know this shit inside out," she said, her voice flat with real anger. "Heard it in the churchhouse, heard it in the schoolhouse, heard it in the flapbox in my own house, heard it up to here." She sliced her hand across her throat. "And you telling me again? What the fuck for?" She slid her chair back and stood. "Tell me I got hands. Tell me I got feet."

"Clean," I said.

"Fuck you, Freddie. Your world's got no place to shit. You fuck it up by being there." She walked to the door, opened it, leaned on it. "This much is mine," she said.

I looked around at the wooden chairs and card tables, the strung-out clowns propping up their faces with their bony fists. "You can have it," I said and looked back at Dee, but she was gone.

I caught up with her fifty yards down the street. She was crying. "Tonight," she said, arms around me again, elbows at my ribs, hands on my shoulder blades, breasts pressed tight against my chest. "We do it tonight, together, and I'll go with you."

"I can't. The whole idea . . ."

"Clean," she said. "You do it once with me, and I'll quit."

"Why?"

"No questions." She thudded my chest with the heel of her hand.

"Okay," I said. Even as I said it, I knew I wouldn't.

Lonnie didn't answer the door, but I could hear Steel Pulse on the stereo. I tried the knob. The door was unlocked. Lonnie sat on the floor across the room, arms around his long legs, back against the off-white wall. He was wearing white pants with perfect creases and a soft gray V-neck sweater that gathered at the waist. His eyes focused on the carpet, a blank stare that made him look older than he was and tired, really tired. Even after I closed the door, he didn't look up.

"I found Dee," I said. My stomach jerked just saying it, thinking of the needle. She needed something, like an act of faith, before she could come with me, but I had to think of an alternative, like cutting off an arm or walking barefoot through fire. I wanted to tell Lonnie all this, but he'd say Huck Finn and Nigger Jim, the more I hated her the more I'd love her. "Junkies are dead people," he told me once, while his brother lay in bed in the next room, groaning and sweating through withdrawals. "You can't invest in the dead," he'd said. "You get them back or give them up." Lonnie would want to know why I loved Dee. That was like wanting to know the why of my thoughts, the why of my walk. If my reasons for loving her were bad, I didn't care. I couldn't. Lonnie still just sat, so I said again, "I found Dee."

He nodded, staring at the carpet. His right hand went to his mouth.

I stared at the carpet where he was looking. Nothing was there. "She's going to leave with me."

He moved his head up slowly. "Angela was just here."

"Wilson's Angela?"

"She wanted to borrow money." He lowered his eyes again.

"What's the story, Lonnie?" I squatted to look at him eye to eye. He wouldn't look up. "She with Wilson now?"

His head shook slowly from side to side, eyes still down. "I didn't tell him." His long brown hands covered his eyes, then he raised his head level with mine. "I just gave her the money." He didn't move, hands over his eyes like when we were kids playing hide-and-seek. For a moment, he became a kid, nine years old. I must have become one too, because I looked around the room for a couch to crawl under, a door to squeeze behind.

Just when I expected Lonnie to say "ready or not," he said, "You *know* what she wanted that money for," and dropped his hands. For an instant he must have seen me still as a little boy, because the corners of his mouth pulled back into a surprised smile before falling back into line.

"I thought she was clean. I thought that was the whole point."

"*Was*. She said she kept getting sad." His head started shaking again, back and forth, slowly.

I thought of Wilson in the Coupe de Ville, his long neck curved up, watching the rain explode on the windshield and the people coming and going from the Unemployment building. "You've got to tell your brother," I said.

Lonnie's head stopped moving. He looked me straight on. "No, I don't." His stare was so solid I could feel it on my face, like an open hand, one of Lonnie's big hands across my face. He stood. The hand lifted. "I made her promise to leave town. I wouldn't give her the money until she promised."

I stood next to him. "You trust her?"

"No, I don't *trust* her." He brushed his hand across the rear of his immaculate pants. "You want to come with me?"

"Where?"

"I'm going to get my brother and we're going to eat out, some place expensive, then maybe we'll see a movie, or come here and watch television and smoke, or anything."

"Dee and I . . ."

"Dee can't come."

I nodded. "We've got plans."

Lonnie put his arms around me, pulled me close. "You should come with us, Freddie. I'll buy you a steak."

"I can't," I said.

He leaned back, smiled. "A lobster, then, and I'll introduce you to a woman. Black, if you want black. I even know a very lovely paraplegic who's half Puerto Rican."

Then I surprised myself by putting my arms around Lonnie. "I love Dee," I whispered, right in his ear.

I spent the afternoon with my parents. We couldn't find much to talk about and sat in the TV room watching "Star Trek"—the crew had beamed down to a planet where everyone's dreams came true and all it did was cause them trouble. My parents had moved from the old neighborhood to a trailer park called Happy Trails Trailer Lots. All the mailbox poles looked like hitching posts. My mother said it was very quiet.

Dee had grown up less than a block from where we used to live, but she had never seen the inside of our house until we were in high school. She was quiet around my parents in a way she was with no one else. "They praying I'm a phase," she'd say, once we were out of the house. It became a routine. "Your number 1 phase wants to go dancing," she'd say. "This phase is getting fat and fat phases never last." One night my parents were having a party. I was in the shower when my father barged into the bathroom, drunk. He pulled the curtain aside, saying we needed to talk. I tried to pull the curtain shut again, but he put his arms around me and pressed his face against my chest, even though the water was spraying all over. "Honey," he said, a name he used when he got drunk and sentimental. "She's not just black, she's a nigger. There's a difference." I clubbed him with the soap and he left.

He apologized the next day, the same day Dee made her biggest effort to get next to them. She told a joke about a dog that loses his tail so he has to wag his tongue. Halfway through it, my father said excuse me and left the room. Mother was ironing and never laughed, but went right into a story about a dog we used to have that died under the house and made a stink. Dee quit trying after that.

"Police Woman" was on after "Star Trek." No one liked it, but the TV made it easier for us all to be in the same room. My father got out his needlepoint, which he had taken up after I left. He never wrote letters, but sent ugly needlepoint flowers or doodads and notes mentioning that Rosie Grier did needlepoint. He included the note so I wouldn't think he'd

gone queer. Mother drank her beer and said an actress got
her start on "The Edge of Night."

On TV, a sniper wearing a red ski mask aimed his rifle at a
woman carrying a shopping bag. Right then it hit me that I
was going to have to shoot heroin or lose Dee. I couldn't do
either one. The show became a marker. By the time it was
over, I would have to go to Dee's and do *something*. I could
see the needle pressing against my skin. A little cup in the
flesh formed around the point as the needle pressed in more.
The skin broke, needle sank in, flesh rose around it.

I had to get Dee out of Langston without doing junk. Angie
Dickinson, tied with a yellow extension cord to a chair, wag-
gled her butt to scoot the chair across the floor, closer to the
window. She was being held hostage by the man in the red ski
mask. The show was almost over. I left, trusting my parents to
see how Angie escaped.

Dee named the biggest vein in my arm Mississippi and
pinched it out with her fingers. She sucked the last of her
Pepsi out of the paper cup and set it behind her on the floor.
It caught the edge of a magazine and tipped over, spilling
beads of ice across the faded yellow tile. Her apartment was
one little room in the back of a grocery store. Magazines lit-
tered the floor. A thin striped mattress lay flat in one corner,
partially covered by a dirty pink sheet. A TV rattled on in another corner, but I didn't look. I didn't want to see the needle.
Instead, I looked at a poster, curling at the edges, hanging
crooked on the wall, a picture of the earth taken from space.
The world was blue, streaked with white. It looked like a
great place. Paper-clipped to the poster was a photo of Dee,
Lonnie, and me from our trip to LA to see Bob Marley and the
Wailers. I had my arm around Dee and Lonnie had his arm
around me.

I had delayed as much as I could, talking about my classes,
where we would live, my parents, "Star Trek," how I threw

beer at Eugene, Angela borrowing money from Lonnie. I tried
to distract myself from the needle, couldn't, tried to think of
it as walking barefoot through fire.

I pumped up my arm when Dee told me to. The photograph was dark. We were all smiling. She tied my arm off with
a vinyl belt. I tried to remember the Wailers live. She pinched
out the vein again. "Put some Bob Marley on," I said, head still
turned.

"Traded all I had to Eugene."

"For what?" I asked. Instead of answering, she stuck the
needle in my arm.

My arm tensed hard as wood, but the needle was already
out, the belt off. Something like sleep turned in my chest,
came up my throat on a wave of static, then flooded out all
over. Even my fingers filled with light. "Jesus," I said.

"Our savior," Dee laughed.

I started to turn to her but began yawning. In the TV in the
blue corner: Chef Boyardee, Tony the Tiger, the Shell Answer
Man, the flat yellow hat the laughing blonde presses against
her breasts. Beside the set: a sour gray apple whose skin curls
around a missing piece like lips protecting teeth. A gurgle
from Dee I had to laugh with. Dolphins standing straight up in
the television like children choosing sides for baseball. It was
like a movie, this life. The crushed cup, drained of Pepsi, had
bunches of ice that looked like caviar. I said "caviar" and
slipped a piece into Dee's mouth.

"When *you* ever seen caviar?" She was laughing.

I decided we should make love. Little legs began crawling
across my cheek, but I scratched them off. Dee lay back on
the pink sheet, kissing me once, her lips fibrous as peaches. I
couldn't get it up, even though my currents sizzled like rain
on asphalt, like a scaled fish in salt water.

"You don't need to fuck on junk," Dee said. "You don't
need to do anything."

"I want to," I said. "It's Christmas," meaning we hadn't

made love since I left in December. A fly landed on my face, but it was not a fly. "Is there something on my face?"

She smiled, lit a Kent 100. The smoke came inside my lungs liquid. If you listened to a smoking cigarette, it sounded like TV static, like locusts, like heroin humming through the veins inside your skull.

Dee laughed and that started me laughing. She walked from the mattress to the TV, stepping only on magazines. "Piranhas," she said and pointed to the yellow tile.

I joined her. We stepped from magazine to magazine, as if from stone to stone, above the man-eaters. At the TV, she turned off the sound, abandoned the game, and walked to the stereo. She put on an album of saxophones I didn't recognize, then locked her arms around me. "You do love me," she said.

"I must," I said. My stomach started twisting. Dee led me to the bathroom. I knelt in front of the toilet but didn't vomit. We began dancing to the saxophones, slow at first, then faster, pushing off the walls to send us across the floor faster. We slid on the magazines, and that became part of the step.

I began throwing up and that became part of the dance too. We were both laughing. She kissed me hard. Our tongues became part of the dance. Vomit trailed across her mouth and down her cheek. We danced back to the mattress and pulled at each other's clothes. The music was over, maybe for a long time.

I kissed her breasts, bit her ribs. My fingers sank into the soft of her butt. "Freddie," she said, and I raised my head. "We can really get out?" I kissed her again, wiped the vomit from her face. "Freddie," she said again.

"We can get out," I said. "Eight hundred miles." I entered her. We made love for what may have been a long while. And all the time, inside the frenzy was the calm. Memory hovered about my head, becoming visible at intervals, like particles of dust in twilight—the alley behind the Bree where we bought pot, beneath the slide in the Woodard schoolyard where Dee and I first made love, the corner of 5th and Main where the knobby prostitutes hawked, the vacant lot behind the Mesa Drive-In where we made up dialogue for the huge silent screen, all the places we grew up lost—the men in suits and vests with high-polish shoes, the bearded transvestite who collected bottles in the basket of his bicycle, the black butcher with red slabs of meat, the abandoned Sinclair station covered with names, my name, Dee's, Lonnie's, Wilson's, Eugene's—the curtains of my parents' house drawn closed, the liquor store on 49th with the neon dinosaur, the all-night diner on 4th Avenue, Lonnie's Coupe de Ville, the asphalt bedrooms, the Unemployment building, my mother, who told me the last people who lived here didn't know how to behave.

"It's like dancing in the movies," Dee said, her hand on my chest. She laughed, looked confused. "Did I already say that?" She pulled gently at my dick. "I love you, Freddie. A lot. A very lot."

We slept.

"She just wasn't there," I said to Lonnie. The windows were starting to go dark and no sign of Dee all day. My head was clear, arm a little sore, and that grown-up feeling, age that just fell into me like a brick into a pond. Not that I liked needles or wanted junk, but I knew I couldn't tell Lonnie about heroin ever, and knowing that put a distance between us, made me feel older. "I slept late and she was just gone."

"You know where she is." He was on the floor, propping himself up with his elbows. Lonnie always sat on the floor if he had a choice.

"I know what she's doing. I don't know where she is."

Lonnie let his head drop back. He had the same long neck as his brother. He and Wilson had eaten last night across town, then drank beer at the Mesa Drive-In, laughing and watching James Bond. All the tension Lonnie had the night before was gone. His brother was at a local concert in memory of Bob Marley. Lonnie believed he was safe, at least for the night. He lifted his head, smiled at me, straightened his black pinstripe shirt. "We'll look for her," he said. "Then we'll put you both on a bus."

We drove the old streets, checked the regular spots—like the old times, me and Lonnie cruising, looking for familiar cars, waiting for something to happen. There was no sign of Dee. We decided to try the reggae concert, although neither of us thought she would have the money for it. On our way, Lonnie spotted Eugene's old Chrysler parked on a dark stretch of 32nd Street. We cut around and pulled up to the car.

A Mexican with long frizzy hair lay on the hood of the Chrysler. Eugene sat behind the wheel, hand tapping the dash. Beside him, the dog-faced junkie from the Bree. "Don't stop," Eugene said as we pulled up next to the car. "We waiting here. You can't stop."

"You seen Dee?" I leaned over next to Lonnie, tried to see in the car.

"No, no, fuck." Eugene looked in his rearview mirror. Headlights appeared from around the corner, then stopped a hundred yards before reaching the cars. "She ain't here, come on." His hand hammered the dash faster.

I started to ask again, but Lonnie pulled out, U-turned so we didn't go by the other car. "Let them be," he said. "Let them rest in peace."

The headlights neared Eugene's car. A head rose from the backseat of the Chrysler. "There's somebody in the backseat," I said.

Lonnie shrugged. "Doesn't mean it's Dee. Besides, we can't stop what's going on there."

The reggae concert was in an old warehouse and was sold out. From the outside, all we could hear was the bass. I tried to imagine it as part of a song, but it distorted everything. We drove again. Lonnie produced a joint. I only smoked a little.

The night was dark, sky empty. I remembered something from the night before. "Let's go to the old Sinclair station," I said.

"They tore it down," Lonnie said.

We drove out on the loop we always used to take. I caught Lonnie staring at his reflection in the dark window and we laughed. The neon sign for the Oasis Motel read *as s Mot l*, gas gauge read under a quarter of a tank. Lonnie's car had only AM radio. All we could find was cowboy music and people talking on telephones.

Lonnie turned the radio off. He looked straight ahead, one hand pinching the crease in his pants. "I love you, Freddie," he said, "but you're not strong enough. She'll drag you down. It's dirty, Freddie. It's ugly."

I turned to him, opened my mouth to speak, and suddenly I realized why Dee had wanted me to shoot heroin. She had to see if I could be strong, if I could do the thing I hated most *for her*. It hit me so hard I almost told Lonnie, so I would never hear about Huck Finn and Nigger Jim again. Instead, I said, "I can be stronger than you think."

We turned back.

Lonnie took 5th. It was mainly residential, good at night because there was never any traffic and no cops. He wanted to smoke another joint. I fumbled through the glove box to find one. The yards were green all year round, trimmed straight to give them edges. I lit the joint just before we reached 5th Street Park, a big grassy area with trees and swings. A car pulled out of the park and approached with its lights off. As it passed, I recognized Eugene and his beat-up Chrysler. I tried to see who else was in the car but couldn't make out anyone. Lonnie just shrugged.

As we drew nearer to the park, I saw a dark mound in the grass twenty yards from the street. I pointed. Lonnie stopped the car. We looked at it through the windshield. It didn't move. I couldn't tell whether the mound was a man or a woman. Lonnie cut the engine. The night was perfectly quiet.

Fear entered me like heroin had, turning in my chest, filling me. I hoped it was that dog-faced junkie from the Bree or the Mexican who had lain on the hood of Eugene's Chrysler or someone I had never seen or heard of. I felt like we should run to it, but we walked close to one another, very slowly.

"No," Lonnie said. "No, no."

Wilson's head twisted to the side, vomit was spattered across his chin, shoulder.

We squatted beside the body. Lonnie began crying. Neither of us wanted to touch the body, but one of his arms was wrenched behind his back. I couldn't leave him that way. I pulled on the arm at the elbow.

The arm jerked, eyelids rose. "Hey, brother," Wilson said. He smiled a goofy smile and lifted himself up on his elbows.

"Jesus," I said. "We thought you were dead."

"I puked all over Eugene's car," he said, still smiling.

Lonnie raised his hand and slapped Wilson hard. He was still crying, trembling.

Wilson just fell back. "I'm sorry," he said.

Lonnie stood, one hand over his eyes. He brought up the other to cover his mouth.

I kissed Lonnie on the cheek, a love kiss, but not a lover's kiss.

"She promised she'd leave," Lonnie said.

"You can't blame Angela for this," Wilson said, up again on one elbow. "Angela?" he called out. He turned to the dark and vacant park. "Angela?"

The bus out of Langston moved like a sick dog. Dee, in the window seat, looked at the same streets she'd seen all her life. The early morning light made everything look fake, like movie scenery. We went by the liquor store on 49th, the neon dinosaur flickering blue, past the grocery store Dee lived behind, still lit by its nighttime lights. Eugene squatted next to the grocery door. His back partially covered the diagonal yellow band advertising bread. WONDER, the sign read.

Dee put her head on my shoulder. "I guess this street don't owe me nothing I ain't already took."

I put my hand on her cheek. She had been sleeping on the porch of Lonnie's apartment when we pulled in. We had taken Wilson inside, then I woke her. "Eight hundred miles," she had said, high on junk but ready to go. And we were going. I tilted our seats back and closed my eyes.

"Your place have carpet?" Dee asked. "I hate carpet."

"We can pull it out," I said.

"It's a few things I can't tolerate and carpet's one."

"You don't have to talk," I said. "I'm too tired to laugh."

She kissed my cheek and we rode on, but I couldn't sleep. I didn't want to think about Lonnie and Wilson starting over again and again or about Eugene sitting in the Chrysler beating the dash, waiting for headlights. I didn't even want to think about me and Dee—it made me tired. And scared.

I tried again to hear Bob Marley, but his music just wouldn't come. I pictured him on stage in the blue light with the silver mike. Instead, I saw him skinny in some hospital bed, shitting in his sleep, his breath already the color of death, thinking, *It all comes down to this moment*, trying to say what was left inside, what hadn't been strangled by the white hands of cancer. I tried to hear Marley's words and wondered if the vision grew soft before the mind or the mind before the vision.

Then I heard Bob Marley.

His voice was nothing like the living Marley's voice. It was flat, even, without any Jamaican accent. "Bury the swollen tongues of the dead," he said, and I understood that the faith of the living was with the dead and the faith of the dead with the living.

The bus rattled across a hole in the road, then lugged as it entered the freeway. Dee slept. The driver downshifted. We picked up speed. The sky grew light but without color, like concrete. I looked at Dee and she opened her eyes.

"Shh," she said, then fell back to sleep.

The Darkness of Love

THE DARKNESS OF LOVE

The darkness of love,
in whose sweating memory all error is forced.

—Amiri Baraka

DAY 1

When Handle woke at ten in the morning, he got up and walked to the far window. Hung over, he half expected the sound of traffic or the fading drone of an airliner as he lifted the window. He had lived in the city for so long that even after two weeks in Tennessee, he found the quiet of the green countryside severe and foreign. Trees just appeared outside his window, new, each morning. He had come to escape the city, but his dreams returned him each night to New York, sometimes in a patrol car but most often on his feet, in an alley, running after a bone-skinny black boy who would suddenly turn, knife in his hand, and Handle would wake, startled that the boy's face was his, a younger face, but essentially his.

Handle dressed in the corduroy jeans he'd bought for the trip and pulled a blue T-shirt with white lettering over his head. His wife had given him the shirt, which read HANDLE WITH CARE. He walked back to look at the trees again. Wind through the leaves sounded like people speaking, and the sound of voices made him feel more at home. He closed the window quietly, as if the noise would disturb the trees, the grass, or his in-laws, who, he was sure, had been awake for hours.

As he turned from the window to his unmade bed, he pictured his wife stealing a few minutes' extra sleep, waiting for him to kiss her neck and shake her awake. The image of her brown body against the white sheets sparked a memory—a night before they were married. He had promised to meet her in the lobby of an auditorium and was running late. In the dim lights of the smoke-filled lobby, he'd had trouble finding her. Finally he spotted her across the room, leaning against the wall opposite him. That was the memory: Marilyn, tall, thin, dark against the white stucco wall, wearing a thick beige coat fringed with fur, staring into the crowd with an expression of anticipation and melancholy. At that moment, she looked as beautiful as anyone he'd ever seen. When she saw him crossing the lobby, she smiled and moved to meet him. But that whole evening, as Handle saw it, revolved around that one frozen image of his future wife leaning against a wall, looking sad, beautiful, eager.

Handle had spent the past two weeks with Marilyn's parents, trying to relax, with mixed results. He'd enjoyed the time but couldn't escape the nagging discontent that had driven him away from the city, his home, his wife. Louise, Marilyn's sister, had arrived from Los Angeles two days ago, giving him someone else to talk to. She'd just completed her second year of law school. Marilyn would finish her finals today, and by tomorrow she would be in Tennessee as well.

"You sleep later every day," his sister-in-law said, smiling at him as he walked down the stairs. Louise's eyes had always fascinated him, the same light brown as her skin but luminous.

He grinned at her. "I might have had a little too much to drink last night."

"That's safe to say." She waited for him to say something more, then moved her hands from her hips to her shoulders, crossing her arms. In one hand she held a book of Emily Dickinson. "You've missed breakfast, but if you talk really sweet, I *might* be persuaded to warm up the biscuits and make some gravy."

"Too early for me to think about food," Handle said, thinking how tired he was of milk gravy and flat biscuits. He thought he'd like a steak, a New York cut, but he smiled at his lovely sister-in-law. "Maybe later, Louise."

"Later will be too late." She laughed and walked out of the room. Handle watched the swish in her hips and knew he'd been away from his wife too long. But, then, the way Louise walked had always interested him. Her hips rolled like the shoulders of a swimmer.

He and Marilyn had been married six months when he'd first met Louise. The two sisters had walked in the front door of the apartment, each carrying suitcases and laughing. Louise's beauty had shocked him: her eyes, her walk, the trace of Tennessee in her voice that seemed to come and go as she wished. He thought of his wife again, her handsome face and long, angular body. He knew being away from her made Louise seem more appealing. Her presence always kept his interest in Louise in perspective.

He walked into the kitchen, took a bottle of orange juice from the refrigerator, and brought the bottle to his mouth. Orange juice and aspirin were key ingredients in his favorite hangover cure.

"Wayne Handle, we have glasses in this house, and I wish you'd use one."

Handle looked at his mother-in-law, standing with her hands on her hips just as Louise had stood earlier. That posture must run in the family, he thought. "Good morning, Annalee," he said and took another swig of orange juice. He noticed the flyswatter in her hand. "Kill anything yet?"

Her face lost its sternness. "I ought to kill you, drinking all night, telling foolish stories, sleeping the lifelong day away. What am I going to tell Marilyn when she gets here? That her husband's been acting like some teenage boy?" She giggled and the sound reminded Handle of his wife. "If you'd told that story about the alligator one more time, we'd have all shot you." She laughed out loud.

"They made me do it."

"Louise and Marvin are gluttons for punishment." Annalee laughed again and walked out the screen door into the sunlight. Another inherited trait, he thought: wandering off to end a conversation. He looked out the screen door just as

Annalee brought her flyswatter down on the leg of her husband, who had been dozing in the porch swing. Marvin never lifted his head but raised his huge left arm and swatted Annalee on her behind. Who's the teenager? Handle wondered.

Before he'd met his in-laws, Handle had heard a story that had shaped his opinion of Annalee and Marvin. Their old dog, Hoot, had gone blind. Marvin speculated it stemmed from eating inky cap mushrooms, but Annalee insisted age had blinded the yellow dog. Too old to adjust, Hoot would become confused in the big yard, howling until someone came after him. He began shitting in the living room and lifting his leg on the furniture. Marvin couldn't bear the thought of putting Hoot to sleep. He'd found the dog as a pup, cradled in the boughs of the purple magnolia that marked the northeast corner of their property. Who put the dog there and why, they never discovered, but Marvin attached significance to finding a puppy in a tree. Annalee finally solved the problem. She made a trail with bacon grease from the front porch to the old barn where he like to pee, to the thick grass near the purple magnolia where he liked to shit, and back to the porch. The old dog ran this circle the last two months of his life. When he finally died, Marvin insisted they bury him under the purple magnolia. Annalee dug the hole and buried the dog. The tree promptly died, leaving Marvin to speculate on the connectedness of all living things. Annalee argued that she may have severed the taproot while digging the grave, but Marvin ignored her.

Just as Handle turned away from the screen door, Marvin's thick voice boomed across the porch. "Handle, come quick. This woman's getting feisty. I need you to tell her that alligator story again." He paused as Annalee started laughing. "That ought to calm her down."

Handle yelled back through the screen. "I was on patrol, first year on the force . . ."

"Aggh." Annalee swatted Marvin one last time and ran into the yard with her hands over her ears. Handle's laughter hurt his head, and he decided to go to the bathroom to search for aspirin.

Four aspirin were left in the bottle. Cupping his hand under the running faucet, he swallowed all four. As he lifted his head from the sink, his face rose in the mirror on the medicine cabinet, a dun-brown face several shades drabber than when he'd left the city. His eyes appeared yellow. He cupped his hands again and slapped his face with cold water. Running his fingers through his hair, he parted it at just the spot where his teeth parted, in the middle. Twice during his stay, Annalee and Marvin had cut off arguments when they heard him approach. He realized they were acting especially cheerful for his benefit, going out of their way to make him feel comfortable, knowing he must be in some kind of trouble to have come to Tennessee alone. He wanted to give them something in return, the thing they needed—an explanation.

He wanted to tell them that his job had become too much, that the ugliness and violence of being a cop had become overwhelming. He believed that would be adequate. They could nod their heads knowingly or shake them sadly, then relax, even quarrel with him if they wanted. Better yet, if he could give them an incident—perhaps he'd killed a man in self-defense—they could forgive and console him. However, the incident he had to tell was neither violent nor vulgar, but he had been unable to deal with it and unable still to discuss it.

It had happened in a bar. Off duty, he'd waited for a friend who had tickets for the Mets. As he drank a beer and looked over the bar, he noticed a kid in the booth directly behind his barstool, a black kid, fairly young, whom he recognized as some kind of offender. He couldn't place the kid, but he'd seen the face connected with something serious. Across the booth from him, another boy, white and very young, squirmed in his seat. He could tell something was going on under the table, probably passing drugs.

Handle tried to watch them without being seen. He didn't

know exactly what was happening or where he'd seen the black kid, but he had no doubt the kid was trouble. He could just tell. The bartender brought him another beer. As he looked up to pay for it, he noticed a mirror with a Budweiser ad and, in it, the kid, his lap, and a white hand groping his crotch. Even then, knowing they weren't dealing in anything but each other, Handle couldn't shake the feeling that the kid was no good.

His friend finally arrived, another cop, white, mumbling that there was enough time for another beer. "Turn around slow," Handle said. "The black kid in the booth, who is he?"

His friend looked, then turned back, shaking his head. "Don't know him, but he looks something like that Jenkins kid who was shot last week. You remember," he said, "that shit who stabbed women through the ribs as he raped them."

Handle became frightened, turning around so quickly that he knocked over his beer and startled the kid. The boy looked him straight in the face, and Handle could see he resembled the Jenkins boy some. He had the same high cheekbones, the same uplifted upper lip, the same empty stare, and he was black, most of all he was black.

Handle tried to ignore the incident, go on with his life, but he'd lost his edge, questioned too many decisions and motivations, discovering that he looked at black men a little harder than at whites. He knew the phrase for it: *he had an eye out for bad niggers.* Finally, he'd told Marilyn he needed to get away, even though she had two weeks of school left. She'd seen his uneasiness and seemed relieved that he could point to his job as the problem. Handle, however, couldn't tell her that he thought of himself as a racist.

He rinsed his face again with cold water and walked out of the bathroom. Across the hall, in the walk-in closet under the stairs, Louise tried to pull sheets from the top shelf. As she stretched for the sheets, her white muslin dress rose to her thighs, revealing her white underwear and the curves of her bottom. Handle thought of the summers she'd spent with them in New York. Once that first summer he had come home early, a little shaken from a scuffle with an afternoon drunk, and found her and Marilyn naked on the patio playing cards. "Expecting someone else?" he'd asked. Marilyn had been startled, but Louise laughed and reached behind her for her dress. Then she had been a year away from completing college. Now she was a year away from becoming a lawyer. Always something about her was unresolved.

Louise turned with the sheets in her hands and caught him staring. "You scoundrel," she said with a hint of accent. She threw the sheets at him. "You could have helped me out."

"It was more fun watching." He caught the sheets and threw them back. The top sheet inflated as it flew.

She laughed and stumbled as the sheets caught her full in the face. "Wayne Handle, you're the most worthless man I know."

He waited for her to pull the sheets from her face so he could see if that stern look was there, to see if that was an inherited trait as well as the habit of using his full name. But she lunged at him, pushing the sheets over his head, laughing as she knocked him off balance and they both fell to the hard-wood floor.

He pulled the sheets off his head, looked at Louise sprawled face down at his feet, her dress up to her waist. Her body bounced with its own laughter. The throb of his headache quickened as he laughed. She sat up quickly and straightened her dress. "Worthless," she said, smiling. "Worthless."

A drizzle began in the afternoon and became a full-fledged rain before dark. At dusk, with stomachs full of mashed potatoes and mutton, the family sat in separate chairs on the porch and watched the rain fall. Handle thought the rain looked like pencil lines on cheap paper. For a moment he pictured himself in the first grade, his fat red pencil in his hand,

copying the alphabet from the cards over the blackboard. He
remembered Mrs. Hayes, his first-grade teacher, stalking the
aisles with her ruler to swat anyone caught talking. Handle
realized he was smiling. The image of that old woman, her
white hair hovering around her black head like a cloud,
seemed comical. But she had taught him how to read. In her
class he had decided to become a teacher. He wondered
when he'd lost track of that.

"There's nothing like rain, except maybe fire, that can hold
a body for hours, just watching it," Marvin said. Marvin was so
large that any chair he sat in was too small. Handle remembered his own father sitting in one of the first-grade desks,
waiting to have a word with Mrs. Hayes, wanting to see if she
could teach him to read the way she'd taught his son. The image of his father faded. Both Marvin and Annalee had taught in
rural Tennessee schools. Handle had wanted to talk with
them about teaching, but he'd never told anyone he'd wanted
to be a teacher and couldn't bring himself to share his secret
with them.

He looked back at the rain and picked up his bottle of beer.
"The ocean," he said, feeling the cold bottle in his hands. "I
could stare at the ocean all day." Handle pictured a wave
coming toward him, looking like a cupped hand which would
flatten just before reaching him.

"I've heard people say that," Marvin said.

"I can look at stars that way," Annalee said. "Nights without
a moon."

Each of them turned to Louise, waiting for her to complete
the circle of conversation. She said nothing, sitting with her
legs tucked under her body, staring at the rain.

"Darling," Annalee said, looking at her daughter, "I've seen
you staring at a man's bottom so long and hard I'd have sworn
it was going to fall off."

Marvin smiled, Annalee and Handle laughed. Louise forced
a smile, then let it fade. "Words," she said. "I can look at

words on a page until they seem to glow." Handle could see the shine in her eyes.

"You always loved books," Marvin said. "I've never seen a child take to books so young."

Handle's eyes hadn't left Louise. Something about her sitting there, staring off into the darkening sky, her hair with drops of rain like jewels—he became afraid that he was falling in love, or that he had been in love since that first summer and had never admitted it, that he might scoop her up in his arms, here in front of her parents, and carry her to the room where he slept and make love with her. He tried to shrug off the feeling, staring out into the rain and reminding himself that Marilyn would be back by tomorrow night, and such thoughts would seem silly to him. But he couldn't resist looking back at her.

"Louise," Annalee said, rising from her chair, "you want to help with the dishes?"

Handle didn't want Louise to move. "I'll help you, Annalee," he said. As he stood, he heard Louise's voice, as if coming from a long distance, "Thank you."

Handle washed and Annalee dried. The window over the sink became covered with steam, and the sound of rain filled the room. Annalee hummed a tune Handle recognized but could not remember. He liked the feel of the hot water on his arms and hands, but Louise's eyes, her voice, hung in his mind.

"Will Marilyn need four years to get her degree?" Annalee ran a towel in circles over a dish.

"She could make it in three if her old classes transfer. Why?"

"Just wondering," she said and began humming again.

"What's that you're humming?"

She stopped, thought for a moment, then laughed. "Why, I don't know. I was just humming away, but as soon as you asked it left me. What did it sound like?"

Handle laughed. "Something like a cat in heat."

Annalee slapped his shoulder with the dish towel. "You shouldn't be mean to your mother-in-law. You don't talk that way to Marvin, and you're sure not mean to Louise."

Handle handed her another dish. He smiled but felt suddenly uneasy, wondering if his feelings toward Louise might be more obvious than he'd thought. He tried to discard the notion and concentrate on the dirty pot in his hands. They worked for a few moments to the sound of rain before Annalee started humming again.

She stopped abruptly. "Georgia on My Mind."

"Ray Charles," Handle said.

"Now that's out of the way, I'm going to ask you straight out, Wayne Handle."

Handle felt his stomach tense, afraid she might say something about Louise.

"Are you and my daughter going to have children?"

His stomach relaxed, but he didn't really know how to answer the question. "Marilyn's got to finish school."

Annalee stared at him for a second, then nodded. "School's a wonderful thing. Between Louise and Marilyn, I'm going to have the most educated daughters in Tennessee—if they were in Tennessee." She put the dish in the cupboard and took the pot from Handle. "The only thing I'd worry about is if Marilyn *did* get pregnant, Louise might run out and do the same, married or not." The screen door opened and Marvin walked through the kitchen to the living room, smiling at them as he passed. Annalee watched her husband, then turned back to the cupboard. "At least there'd be a few little ones around."

"While I'm in town tomorrow, I ought to buy you a puppy," Handle said. "Maybe two." He smiled at her, but she wasn't really amused. "Annalee, that's your dream, not ours."

She smiled weakly and patted his arm. "I know, sweetheart."

Handle put his arm around her in a half hug, but a new question formed for him: what was their dream? He finished the few remaining dishes, and Annalee shooed him out of the kitchen. The rain still fell steadily and Louise hadn't moved, feet tucked under her body, watching the darkness of evening fall with the rain. Talking with Annalee about his wife had diffused the charge that Louise carried. Handle took the chair next to her and looked off into the sky just as a flash of lightning painted a crooked path between dark clouds.

"Daddy's gone to bed," Louise said.

Handle nodded but looked past her to the rain. A thin stream of water dripping from the corner of the roof caught the light and looked like a long strand of twisting tinsel.

"We're all a little worried about you," Louise said.

Finally someone had just said it, Handle thought, but he didn't know what he could say in return. He might tell her that their worry showed in the kindness they extended him, but that sounded patronizing and avoided the question. Besides, he considered that the generosity of the family made it even more difficult to talk. When he'd first met Marvin and Annalee, he'd resented their marriage, believing it made Marilyn expect too much. Now, they'd been so careful to create an atmosphere of goodwill that to introduce his problems into the household seemed ugly and ungracious. Looking at Louise's patient face, he gave the most honest answer he could. "I don't think I can talk about it."

"Have you talked with Marilyn?"

"I wanted to." He folded his arms and looked back at the rain. "I thought once or twice this past week I might talk with Marvin or Annalee. I can't seem to do it."

"Is your marriage in trouble, Handle?"

He looked at her again, the soft curves of her cheek, the light brown of her eyes, then shook his head from side to side. "Sometimes I get this feeling. Riding in a patrol car with some white jackass, I get this queasy feeling, and I wonder who I'm trying to fool. I always convince myself it's better there's one cop who doesn't want to bust black heads, even when he has to. Now I believe that's just what they want me to think."

Louise still stared at him, waiting. He knew she wouldn't settle for an answer so general, but he couldn't tell her more. He stared back at her and found himself watching the minute changes in her face, how her eyebrows lifted and curved back to their normal shape as she moved from waiting for a response to a different attitude. Her eyes became slightly moist. Her lips moved almost imperceptibly as if mouthing a whisper. They sat quietly on the porch for several moments, just looking at one another while the rain fell.

"Oh, Handle," Louise said very softly. "What are you doing here without Marilyn?"

Handle felt something collapse inside him. He told her about the bar and the boy, the white groping hand, and that face, that blank brown face; he told her about the realization he'd come to about himself and how it had affected his work and his life. He spoke quickly, anxiously, watching her face, wondering what she would think of him. She listened patiently, but without giving away her thoughts. When Handle finished the story, he paused, but Louise said nothing and he didn't feel comfortable with the silence. "The department was all right. They know cops get crazy sometimes if they can't get away. And Marilyn understood or thought she did. She believed I needed to get away from dealing with rapists and pimps and junkies. I let her believe that. I didn't know how to tell her the truth."

"Why can't you tell her what you just told me?"

He tried to think of the real answer. Why had he been able to tell Louise what he couldn't tell his wife or her parents? What quality had he invested in her that he hadn't in the others? Perhaps it was just the moment, he thought. But looking at her again, he couldn't believe that was true. "I always wanted to be a teacher. Can you imagine that? I never told anyone. I wanted to teach kids to read."

Louise reached over and put her hand on his arm. "That

first summer I met you, I don't know if you remember this, but Marilyn's friend was pregnant. She was your neighbor. I can't remember her name."

Handle nodded.

"When she miscarried, it was so awful. We thought she might die, the bleeding was so bad, and she was hysterical."

"I remember," Handle said.

"By the time you got home from work, she was hospitalized, but Marilyn and I were wrecks—we were scared. You were so good that night, Handle. You were so strong. I . . . ." She stopped and stared at his face as if what she was about to say was written there. Then she closed her eyes. "You'll get over this," she said flatly.

Handle waited for her to open her eyes. He heard the screen door open, turned, and saw Annalee looking back at them. Only then did he realize Louise's hand was still on his arm.

"Still raining, I see," Annalee said in a voice barely above a whisper.

Handle nodded. The hand on his arm felt hot as an iron. Annalee walked by them to the porch swing. As she walked by, Louise lifted her hand and opened her eyes. The three of them sat without speaking for a long time. The rain fell and Annalee hummed another unrecognizable song.

Handle woke at two in the morning from another dream of the city, of running down an alley after a scared kid and realizing someone was running after him. The quietness of the country dark wakened him further. He pulled on his pants, then sat on the bed another moment, letting his eyes adjust to the dark and his ears to the quiet. He decided to have a beer, sit on the porch, and just listen to the still darkness.

The light from the refrigerator was so stark that the beer didn't look good to him. He took one anyway and started toward the porch. A light shone in the living room and he walked in to turn it off. In the corner of the room, under a lamp, Louise sat in a chair, reading a book. She was wrapped in a gray-blue comforter.

Handle stood in the doorway. "What are you reading?"

She didn't look up at first, finishing something, clearly aware of his presence before he spoke. "Emily Dickinson," she said, then reached out her hand for the beer.

Handle walked over and gave her the bottle, looking at the thin straps that held her white cotton nightshirt in place. "Why are you always reading that woman?"

"Because she wrote like I think, because she loved words for themselves."

Handle squatted to be at eye level with her and took back the beer. "You ought to read black writers," he said. "Richard Wright, Ellison, Baldwin."

"Those are all men. What makes you think I'm more black than I am woman?" She sat up straighter in the chair and turned the light toward the wall so she could see his face without the glare.

Handle looked into her eyes and started to smile, but he could see she was serious. "Because of your past. Because of your parents."

"One of my parents *is* a woman." She spoke without a trace of accent.

"But they're both black." He smiled, hoping the conversation would become less serious.

"Mostly," she said.

Handle lost his smile and moved closer to her. "What's got you talking this way?"

"We've got plenty of white in us, like it or not."

"All right, but who loves you? Who accepts you?"

"Women. The men, black men, white men, they want me, but they don't accept me. You'd be surprised how many men will make fools of themselves trying to get me to go out with them, sleep with them." She looked him in the eyes. "Even you, Handle. You're just like any other man. You look at me and picture me writhing under you, singing out your name."

Handle's first impulse was to deny it, but he stifled the urge, knowing she would just laugh. He felt curiously hurt yet moved, realizing he was seeing Louise clearly for the first time. He'd known her studious side and her playful side, but he'd never seen this part of her before, the part that tried to make the others converge into some meaningful whole.

Louise finally spoke again, looking away. "Besides, I've read all those men, and let me tell you they're more men than black."

Handle said nothing.

"And you, you're more man than you'll ever be black."

Handle straightened his back and furrowed his brow. "I'm a black man."

Louise giggled but stopped; her voice was without laughter. "You're a cop. They pay you to put niggers in jail."

He felt a heavy twist in his throat and an urge to slap her, but he held off. Her face still seemed hard, not phony sternness, but a real hard glare. "Where'd you get this anger, Louise? I've never seen it in you before."

"It's been here," she said, looking down at the book in her lap. "You think men have a corner on anger? All those angry black men you've read got you thinking a woman can't feel anger?"

"But what's made *you* angry?"

"Goddamn you, Handle. Don't you see what it is? You can be so damned stupid."

He waited for her to continue, not knowing what to say, recognizing in himself a familiar, uneasy feeling. An uncomfortable excitement began to build in his chest.

Louise stared down at her hands. "I want to sleep with my sister's husband," she whispered.

Handle put his hand on her cheek and turned her to face him.

"Christ, I hate this," she said. "I never wanted this to happen."

He moved his thumb across her cheek to catch a tear, then

pulled her close. Her arms slowly moved around his body. He became aware suddenly of the quietness of the country. Both fear and desire filled him so that his chest shook to contain them. He clung to her and they sat in the dark for several minutes.

Louise lifted her head and kissed him lightly on the lips, and he found himself kissing her back. "If you weren't Marilyn's husband, I'd make love with you right here, right now. Or if I could just be sure."

Handle stared into her brown eyes and realized their luminous quality was a trace of green that floated in and out of the brown. He pressed his lips against hers and felt her tongue moving across his teeth. He pulled back and saw more tears running down her face.

"If I could be sure," Louise said. She shook her head from side to side. "Handle, I don't know whether I want you in spite of the fact you're Marilyn's husband or *because* you're her husband. If I could be sure, I don't think anything would matter." She put her hand behind his head and pulled him to her. They kissed, and she let her head fall against his chest.

The warmth of her face against his chest both saddened and excited him. He wondered if part of his desire was because she was Marilyn's sister. He didn't want to believe it was that ugly. They sat in the darkness for several minutes. Handle took a deep breath and held it, trying to calm himself. He didn't want to act without thinking, without trying to make sense of what he was feeling. It had been an emotional night, he told himself. Without his wife, he had turned to her sister. Tomorrow Marilyn would be back, and his feelings toward Louise would return to what they had been before.

He wanted to tell her this, tell her that what they were feeling was loneliness and a shared pain brought into focus by their friendship, that this and not love motivated them. Looking at her in his arms, he wavered, wondering what love was if not this. But he resolved to tell her that as much as they longed for each other, they shouldn't make love, that her sister would be here tomorrow and change what they believed they were feeling.

Before he could tell her, she lifted her head, brushed her lips across his cheek, stood slowly, and walked out of the room to her bed. Handle listened to her feet on the stairs and her bedroom door opening and closing. He waited a few moments, then walked into his room.

DAY 2

Handle slept late again. When he woke, he lay in bed listening. On the porch, Marvin sang to himself, a song Handle couldn't quite make out. He heard the noise of water running through the pipes and pictured Annalee washing the dishes after breakfast. He wondered about Louise. Was she still sleeping? Was she reading? He wondered if words sometimes appeared before her face, in bold print, independent even of paper.

He walked to the window and looked out at the trees, suddenly becoming aware of a memory he'd long forgotten. He believed it was his oldest memory, yet he visualized it clearly, as if it were happening. He stands on his mother's huge bed, his hands on the oak headboard, looking out the window, beyond the salt cedar's branches. A hen blown into the pond flaps its wings, claws the water, as thick misting rain shadows the yard and forms large clear drops on the boughs of the tree.

Handle wondered about the memory, its significance, because it seemed important, although he knew the event itself was unimportant. He couldn't even believe something of consequence about his life was tied up in the image. It was the clarity of the memory. He remembered it as if, for an instant, time had puddled and a moment passed before the flow resumed. He held on to the picture a few more seconds, then let it go.

He showered and dressed, paying special attention to his

hair. He shaved and covered his neck with sweet-smelling aftershave lotion, unsure whether this care was for his wife whom he hadn't seen in two weeks or for her sister.

He loved his wife, but there had been times when he felt the need of another woman, when he found it inconceivable to think that he'd never make love to any woman but Marilyn. During such times women inevitably seemed available and desirable, but Handle had never had an affair. The conflict had nothing to do with his love for Marilyn. He needed the security of their marriage. But he also wanted to throw himself into relationships, to be consumed by the many and various women he desired. For years Louise had siphoned off those desires harmlessly. Their flirtatious friendship had stabilized his marriage.

Down the stairs, he heard Marvin still singing. "On the run all night, on the run all day . . ." Handle laughed.

Annalee's voice came through the open kitchen door. "Is that finally you, Handle?"

"I'm finally me." He stepped into the living room and looked into the corner where Louise sat with a book in her hands. "What is it today?" he asked softly.

She looked up at him solemnly, then smiled. "Gwendolyn Brooks, have you read her?"

He shook his head. "Never heard of her." Louise turned back to her book, and Handle tried for a moment to picture her as she had been last night, resting in his arms. Instead, he saw her once again on the porch with drops of water glistening in her hair. Their flirtatious friendship was over, he realized. The confessions of the past night had ended it. They would have to find a new way to deal with one another.

He walked out onto the porch. Clouds obscured much of the sky, but the sun still shone brightly. Perspiration formed along his forehead as soon as he stepped outside. Marvin stopped singing as Handle closed the screen door.

"Trains," Marvin said. His shirt had damp splotches at the armpits and the center of his chest.

"What about them?"

"My father could sit in the Chicago switching yard and watch trains come and go all night." Marvin smiled but his eyes were distant. "They meant something more to him than they ever did to me. I don't know exactly what. Freedom maybe. Adventure."

"Direction," Handle said, surprised at the sound of his voice. He pictured the tracks, the black ties and heavy rails. He liked the image, its solidity. And the train, he pictured the train moving down the tracks with its remarkable conviction. The image became so strong that he barely heard Marvin reply.

"Maybe. Direction's a hard thing to come by."

Handle intended to walk in the woods. The afternoon rains had kept him inside too much and the anticipation of Marilyn's arrival made him restless, so he decided to explore the woods before the sky darkened. A long field of new corn separated the woods from the house. The knee-high stalks had been recently thinned and weeded, hoed-out as Marvin called it, creating an appealing symmetry about the plants and rows.

Handle walked through the corn, inhaling the fragile odor of the green stalks and looking ahead at the woods. Perhaps the mud discouraged him, accumulating around the edges of his tennis shoes so that he had to stomp it off or lift his feet high and walk like a man in snowshoes. But the woods would be drier than the plowed rows and his shoes were already too muddy to wear into town to pick up Marilyn, so something else caused him to stop just before the perfect rows ended. He considered the question but couldn't say why.

He straddled a cornstalk, stared into the woods, and tried to think of the names of the trees. Maples he knew, the leaves like stars with winged pairs of seeds that pirouette to earth, but he didn't see any maples. The trees that marked the end of the field might have been sycamores or oaks, beeches or hickories. As long as he didn't know their names, they were just trees, blocking the sun and engendering darkness. Handle turned away from the woods.

As he began his walk back to the house, he spotted Louise leaning against the birdbath behind the barn. She waved as if washing a windowpane. The birdbath was the gray of concrete, the barn the gray of rotting lumber, but Louise's shirt was bloodred, conspicuous in the landscape, making her appear closer than she actually was. She straightened as he walked to her and put her hands in the pockets of her denim cutoffs.

"Why didn't you go in?" She twisted slightly from the waist as she spoke. The tail of her red shirt looped over her wrists.

Handle felt she'd read his thoughts. "Was it that obvious?"

"Marilyn and I used to play in the woods when we were kids." Her eyes left Handle for the woods. "If you go back far enough, there's a hollow. It was our secret place."

She smelled of cigarettes. On the ground next to the birdbath, white cigarette butts lay scattered like a mutilated alphabet. Handle realized he'd never seen her smoke in her parents' home, although she smoked often when she visited New York. The barn hid this spot from the house, and Handle realized that this too was a secret place for her. "I never had a secret place."

"All kids do," Louise said. "You've just forgotten."

A wasp flew by Handle's head. He followed its flight to the eave of the barn. "My father kept a pretty short leash." He looked back to Louise. She still stared out at the woods, and Handle suddenly became uneasy. Sweat gathered at his temples and the base of his jaw. The sheer greenness of the trees, the grass at his feet, became suffocating. Only the corn, the lone stalks separated by rich brown earth, soothed him. They had room to breathe.

Louise began giggling and turned toward Handle. She rested her hands against the birdbath and leaned against it again. "The day after Marilyn got caught in the barn with Bobby Dill—oh, they weren't doing anything. She was only in the eighth grade. But the day after, I took a boy out to our secret spot, the hollow. I couldn't let Marilyn get one up on me." She laughed. "Neither one of us knew what to do when we got there, so I acted mad and screamed terrible, mean things at him, hoping Marilyn or somebody would hear. But the hollow is too far out, no one could hear."

Louise laughed again and dipped her head. Handle laughed with her but still felt edgy. She shook her head. "I always had to outdo Marilyn. I thought I was over that."

Her head was still cast down, but Handle could see her face reflected in the rainwater in the birdbath, coppery and clear. Above them, wasps hummed at the openings of their finger-shaped nests. "When Marilyn gets here," he said, "I'm going to tell her . . ."

"I wouldn't." Louise looked up quickly from the bath.

"No, about my job, why I had to leave."

"I was afraid you meant . . ." She shook her head violently. "Last night on the porch, when you told me about that boy in the bar, I thought about the men I know, so sure of themselves they're blind or just the opposite, like puppies—I think of what I want in a man and I see it in you, but maybe that's not it. Maybe whatever I see in you I make myself want." She turned away from him, rested against the birdbath, and faced the dense trees. "What it really is—I see you and Marilyn happy and I want that. I guess I want to take it from her. It's awful, but it must be the truth."

Handle wanted to tell her she was being too hard on herself, but he didn't want to encourage her to believe she really loved him. At least he didn't think he wanted to. At the same time, he didn't want to believe her desire for him was just rivalry with her sister. In some dark corner of his heart, he wanted her to want *him*. But he also wanted it to be over. He said nothing. For several moments they stared at the fields.

Above them, wasps fanned their mud nests, their whine as electric as the surge of blood.

Louise turned toward him, reached into the birdbath, and withdrew a penny. Waves rippled in circles from the point where her hand entered and left the water, and pennies sparkled beneath them like jewels. She placed one damp penny in his mouth, on his tongue, and put another in her mouth. Handle tasted the tart metal and watched Louise. He remembered the taste from childhood, and suddenly he remembered crawling on top of the bookcase in his parents' living room, pulling open the door to the linen closet that was above the clothes closet, and hoisting himself up. The closet was so high it was never used except by him, his secret place where, with the door just cracked open, he could watch the world from a safe distance. He remembered the narrow view afforded by the cracked door and the thrill of the jump down onto the couch. For a moment, he felt that thrill of the secret fall. He started to tell Louise but decided not to, even though she was the first person ever to find her way there. Instead, he tasted the penny and watched her watch him.

Louise finally took the penny from her mouth and dropped it back into the water. "Pennies," she said and smiled, then walked away from him, around the corner of the barn.

The temperature in Monroe, Tennessee, was close to ninety degrees. Handle sat on the bench outside the tiny bus depot. He had been unable to convince himself that the twenty-minute drive to the city would take only twenty minutes. In New York, he would have run into heavy traffic or an accident blocking the road and would have arrived just in time. But he wasn't in New York, so he sat on the bench to wait for the bus.

He looked up and down the city's main street. The air in Monroe didn't seem real to him. He was more comfortable with sky the color of primer paint. A weimaraner sniffed at his shoes, then walked a few yards away and shit on the concrete sidewalk. A man and a woman, holding hands, crossed the intersection of Manhattan and Magnolia against the traffic light. The man had his shirt off. Tufts of black hair on his shoulders and back made Handle think of haircuts, of having clipped hair down the back of his shirt. The woman watched her feet as she walked, as if they began walking on their own and she just followed, curious and somehow saddened by the asphalt beneath them.

Ten minutes before the bus was due, an unshaven man wearing a checkered coat a full size too large walked next to the bench where Handle sat. He held his arm stiffly behind his back, as if he was twisting his own arm to force himself to speak. He was talking to himself as he walked by Handle. "You never take into consideration the whole heart," he said as he passed the bench.

Handle thought of Amy Hansen, a past neighbor and former friend of Marilyn's. He remembered Amy, pregnant and excited about becoming a mother, spending Saturdays with them while her husband worked driving a bus. Marilyn had wanted a child badly during that period. They discussed it almost every night. After the miscarriage, Amy lost her mind. She feared that one day her head would just fall off her shoulders. A redheaded woman with a beehive hairdo passed Handle's bench. She placed one spiked heel in the dog shit as she walked by. In a way Handle couldn't explain, the woman legitimized Amy's fear. Anything is possible, he thought.

The bus was on time. Marilyn stepped off looking softer and younger than he'd remembered. As he hugged her and kissed her, the constancy of his love for her returned instantly. Only after the feeling returned did he realize it had been gone at all. She was full of conversation about her final exams, her last-minute essay, her longing for him, but as they drove through the Tennessee countryside, Handle began thinking of the night before. He questioned whether he could talk with Marilyn but decided to try.

"I don't like being a cop," he said and looked at her. For an instant she had the same look he'd remembered in the lobby years ago: sad, eager, beautiful. "Most of all, I don't like thinking like a cop."

"I've never known you to think like anyone but Wayne Handle," she said.

"Well, Wayne Handle is a cop."

"So how do cops think?" She took hold of his arm with both hands.

"There are certain types we've got to keep on a short leash," Handle said.

"For instance?"

"For instance, blacks."

Marilyn nodded and looked off down the road. Her parents' farm became visible in the distance. "Sometimes you can feel things you don't really believe."

"But how do you tell?"

Handle watched as her gaze left the approaching farm and found him. He loved her gentle face, her unlined forehead and smooth cheeks, her dark and relentless eyes, the perfect ellipse of her mouth. "I love you, Wayne. Everything else I guess at." She laid her head against his shoulder as he guided the car off the main road toward the white farmhouse. He could see Marvin sitting on the porch, watching them approach.

"I thought for sure you'd be fat by now," Marvin said, stepping down the porch steps to greet his daughter. "But you get prettier every time I see you."

She had to jump to throw her arms around his neck. She laughed as she said, "Hi, Daddy." Handle could hear the drawl beginning to return with her first words.

Annalee came out of the screen door with Louise just behind her. "Oh, Marilyn, we were about to fall apart, waiting for you," her mother said, opening her arms.

Marilyn took a few quick steps to her mother and wrapped her arms around her. "Hi, Mama." Even as she hugged her mother, Handle could see his wife's eyes looking toward Louise. He watched as she burst into Louise's arms, saying, "Loosie, Loosie." Handle had forgotten how much taller Marilyn was, how Louise always looked childlike next to her.

The warmth cut loose in the yard was more than even the sky could bear, and large drops of rain began to fall. "Would you look at that," Marvin said. "These northern women always seem to bring the rain with them."

The rain continued through the afternoon and dinner. It was still raining when the table had been cleared, the dishes done, and Marilyn, Louise, Annalee, and Handle joined Marvin on the porch. Handle and Marilyn sat together, arms around each other.

"I can hardly believe we have the whole family together," Annalee said. "Of course, with daughters at either end of the country, I guess we shouldn't expect it too often, but it is nice we're all here."

"I had a dream about being here," Marilyn said. "I dreamed I was up in my room getting ready for bed. I was grown up, but the room was just like it was when I was little. The bed even had that frilly green bedspread Grandma made for me."

"I still have that bedspread," Annalee said.

"I heard a noise outside and I went to the window. All the stars were falling out of the sky into the yard. I ran down the stairs and out to the yard. When I got close, I could see that the stars were ceramic dolls with blue eyes and clothes of silver. They were beautiful."

Handle kissed Marilyn on the cheek.

"That's a lovely dream," Louise said.

Marvin and Annalee exchanged a long look. "Darling," Annalee began. "How well do you remember Grandmother Perkins?"

"I remember her more from pictures than anything else," Marilyn said.

"You were only four or five when she died. She was silly about you. I guess because you were the only grandchild she lived to see. Anyway, she was always making you things, like that bedspread."

"I never did like that thing," Marvin said.

"And giving you things, spoiling you every chance she got. One of the things she gave you was a doll, a white porcelain doll with blue eyes, and she may have been wearing silver clothes. I don't remember."

"I remember," Marvin said. "That doll had a frilly silver dress on."

"Daddy, I never knew you took an interest in dolls," Louise said.

"I remember because I broke the damn thing. It wasn't a doll made for children anyway, made to look at."

"She'd had it since she was a little girl," Annalee said. "But it had never been played with because her father hated the thing—it was so white and had blue eyes. She saved it for her kids, but Marvin was her only child, so she just hung on to it. I guess she knew she was dying and wanted you to have the doll even though you weren't old enough to take care of it."

"I wasn't old enough either. I dropped the damn thing and Mother was ready to take my head clean off." Marvin laughed. Annalee smiled and patted him on the shoulder. The sound of the rain returned as if it had been quiet while the story was being told.

"It's funny you'd remember that. You were so tiny," Annalee said.

"I didn't remember it," Marilyn said. "I dreamed it."

Marvin grunted. "I wonder why your mind stored that doll away all these years, just to bring it out now."

Handle looked out into the rain and thought of the recurring dreams he had of being chased down the streets of the city. He envied Marilyn for her dream. He thought of Marvin's grandfather telling his daughter to put the doll away. He respected the man for that gesture, however cruel it must have seemed to the little girl who would become Marvin's mother. He looked at his wife and wondered how many white dolls were locked within her, waiting to present themselves unexpectedly. He decided he didn't envy her the dream. It was, after all, just a beautiful nightmare.

The family talked and listened to the rain. They talked about Louise finishing school and Marilyn finally going back to school. They talked about the conversation of two nights ago, how they kept making Handle tell his alligator story over and over while Annalee complained. Marvin's thick voice shook the porch as he imitated Handle finishing the story. "There I was standing on a table in the corner of that rundown dive, with a damn alligator staring at me, looking hungry, and before my partner will call for help he wants to know if it's an alligator or a crocodile." Everybody laughed and drank wine or beer. "An alligator or a crocodile," Marvin repeated and laughed again. Handle wondered if they liked the story because the fool asking the question was white.

"Marvin Perkins, if I hear that story one more time, you'll be wondering whether what hit you was a pot or a pan," Annalee said. "Then you and Handle both'll be sleeping in the woods."

It was nearly eleven when the rain began to dissipate and the family moved inside and to bed.

Who can say why a man full of good food and just enough beer, tired from laughing with people he loves and making love with his wife, cannot sleep? And who can be sure that light is not sometimes detectable even through solid walls? At three in the morning, in the doorway of his in-laws' living room, Handle stared across into the far corner. Louise sat in the armchair, bare-shouldered, wrapped in the gray-blue comforter, hands in her lap with a book of poetry. The low reading lamp shone directly on the book, her brown hands, the folds in the comforter. "Louise," Handle said, his voice a hoarse whisper, almost inaudible. She didn't hear. In the indirect light, her face was like the reflection of a face in a dark window—rounded, softened by the night. Her eyes, cast down, gave her a sleepy look, but below their hoods they were lit like tiny candles.

She either hadn't seen him or chose to ignore him, waiting for him to step forward. He had been sure that Marilyn's arrival would stop his thoughts of Louise. When that didn't happen, he believed that after making love with his wife his desire for Louise would fade. But here he was, confident in his love for his wife, unable to sleep, thinking about her sister. He could still stop. He could walk back up the stairs, crawl across his sleeping wife, and return to the familiar, sleepless dark. Handle stepped backward, out of the room. He pivoted out of the doorway and leaned against the wall. His heart knocked around in his chest like a tennis shoe in a dryer. He closed his eyes, but the figure of her in the chair, wrapped in the comforter, took shape, as if imprinted on his retina.

Handle slid silently down the wall into a squat. Moonlight shone through the window onto the dining table, coating the polished mahogany with white light. On the floor, beyond the table, a half circle of light, scattered at the edges, approached him slowly. He pulled his feet back unconsciously, then he heard a page turn in the next room and dropped to his knees in the light. Crooking his head into the opening, he stared again at Louise, dark ovals shadowing the base of her neck, a black splinter separating her lips. He pulled back, settled flat on the floor, his back against the wall. Moonlight reached the middle of his thighs. He tried to sort out his thoughts, but they came too fast and he couldn't make sense of them. He felt suspended in mid jump, the instant before reaching one side or the other or beginning to fall.

Moonlight found his lap, lit half the doorway. The polished table glowed white, like the surface of a still lake. He tried to

picture just such a lake to calm himself, but the pull of Louise
in the next room permitted him no tranquility. He gripped
the doorjamb backhanded to pull himself up, the throb of
blood in his hand so strong he thought it might pulse red. He
stood in the half-lit doorway, moonlight scattering at his feet.

Louise closed her book and looked up at him. His doubts
fell away almost instantly, his thoughts slowed, and he became calm and sure. For a second, he thought of the conversation of the night before and wondered whether he came to
her as a black man or just as a man. He couldn't answer the
question or even consider it, not that the differences were in-
distinct, but they seemed unimportant. Something larger was
present, something he'd hoped to contain in a secret place
hopelessly small. This time he couldn't tell himself Marilyn's
arrival would make it retreat. It wasn't the flickering of lust or
the simple glow of desire that led him to her, but the total
darkness of love.

He walked toward her but stopped before he reached her
chair. She leaned forward when he stopped. "Does it surprise
you I'm here?" she asked.

"No," Handle said. "It surprises me *I'm* here."

"This was always my favorite place to read, wrapped in a
blanket after everyone had gone to sleep. It was always my
part of the house." She ran her hand down the comforter,
smoothing the wrinkles.

The room went silent. They stared at each other bravely.
Louise lifted her hand to the reading lamp and turned out the
light. Handle took another step forward, feeling a sudden
urge to kneel before her. He squatted, at eye level with her,
gripped the arm of the chair. Her hair smelled like cinnamon.
A shuddering in his chest threatened to topple him. He went
to one knee to balance himself.

"When Marilyn arrived," Louise said, "I knew immediately
how I felt about her. And about you." She put her hand to his
temple, the tips of her fingers resting there so lightly he

couldn't be sure she touched him at all. He became afraid again, afraid she might reject him, afraid she might not. "I love my sister." Her fingers brushed across his cheek and jaw. "I would never do anything *just* to hurt her. When I realized that, I knew I loved you as well, Handle."

He took her hand from his face, cupped it in his hands as if it were a liquid he was about to drink.

"Mama and Daddy are old. They sleep like children," Louise said. "Marilyn was so tired. She won't wake." She opened the comforter and Handle looked at her body, the shapes and angles, the turns and shadows. He worried that Marilyn might wake and find him missing or that Marvin or Annalee might want a glass of milk or a breath of air and discover them. But the time for worry had passed and he was helpless to stop. "Just for tonight," Louise said, coming into his arms.

He kissed her lips, her breasts. He ran his mouth down her neck. As their bodies touched, the world stepped back and they entered a private realm. Handle spread the comforter on the floor and they lay together, holding each other, running their hands lightly over their bodies.

They made love slowly. And as they made love, Handle thought of the boy in the bar with another boy's white hand in his lap, he thought of Annalee and Marvin making love at just this pace, this slow pace. He thought of his wife, exhausted from the bus ride, wine, and lovemaking, sleeping in the dark quiet, and he thought of the dark itself, of his dark skin, of Louise's eyes with their flash of green, of rain falling straight to the earth, of pennies sparkling under rainwater, of Marvin as a little boy watching his father watch the trains in the Chicago switching yard, of a train charging ahead, full speed into the darkness, absolutely confident that the rails will take it home into the light, of Louise, here, with him, right now, making love with him, of this night, this instant.

They made love, and the evening seemed to condense into one moment. Handle held Louise close and kissed her lips, feeling as if the moment had a life of its own and that life beat within them both, independent of the dark world around them. And that, perhaps, was enough, he thought, an interval of clarity, one clear, resonant note that stops momentarily the daily march of events. He dressed slowly. He kissed Louise again and returned to sleep with his wife, confident he had witnessed the movement from now to then tremble, where love was as visible and tangible as the rain.

DAY 3

Although he'd lain awake much of the night, Handle woke feeling strong and refreshed, but when he looked at Marilyn dressing, a haze separated them. She caught him staring. "How did you sleep?" she asked.

He thought he should tell her fine, then thought that was silly, he should tell her the truth, that he'd been awake most of the night. But the real truth was that he'd made love with her sister. He felt awkward, so he shrugged his shoulders and rolled onto his side. His face burned with embarrassment.

"I slept like a child," Marilyn said. She sat on the edge of the bed and laid her hand on his back. "It's so peaceful here."

He didn't want to look at her, so he rooted his head into the pillow. Then he felt ridiculous, making the situation worse by acting guilty. He started to roll over to face her but decided that might be too bold, that if she got a good look at his face she would know. He worked his head into the pillow again, his eyes closed. "Uh-huh, peaceful," he said, but his voice didn't sound right to him.

Marilyn slapped him on the butt. "Wayne Handle, are you going back to sleep?"

What had come over him? He felt panicky with every question. He should turn to her, he thought. No, he should be still. He should be natural, as if nothing had happened. Handle tried to think of a natural thing to do. After a moment of deliberation, he scratched his jaw.

Marilyn resumed dressing. "You're going to sleep your life away."

He felt the slight tip of the bed for each leg as she pulled on her jeans. He heard her stand and zip her jeans, then she was back on the bed again, shifting her weight as she slipped on her socks and shoes. She seemed to be dressing very slowly.

"Should I save you any breakfast?"

He could feel her right above him, but he kept his eyes closed. "No," he said. Then she was breathing down his neck. Her lips pressed against his cheek, liquid and hot. He waited for the sound of the door opening and closing, then opened his eyes a crack to be sure she was gone.

Handle sat up in the bed. He had never been unfaithful to Marilyn and up to now hadn't thought of the past night in those terms. It had seemed different, separate from his life with Marilyn. He believed he'd tried to do what was right in order to be true to Louise, to himself, to love. He closed his eyes and thought of Louise. He remembered the softness of her cheek against his chest, the smell of her body, the rhythm of her breathing, the cinnamon smell of her hair. No, he thought, making love with Louise was as genuine as taking a breath.

When he opened his eyes, he saw Marilyn's negligee draped across the dresser and he lost his surety. He stood and walked to the window. The sky had cleared, and the unobscured sun shone so brightly that it seemed to be answering a question he could not formulate. The low limbs of the trees were calm, but wind whipped through the high branches.

Handle took a long shower and shaved slowly. He thought of Marilyn and their marriage. For an instant, he thought he should take her aside and suggest they have children, but he knew the idea grew out of fear and guilt. He wondered whether he was afraid of losing her or just afraid of her knowing he'd betrayed her. He had believed that his lovemaking with Louise had a certain purity, a clarity that transcended convention. But he knew he couldn't explain that to Marilyn and knew that although he'd been honest with himself and Louise, he'd betrayed Marilyn nonetheless. He cupped his hands under the faucet and took a drink. The swallow of water felt like a stone in his throat.

He dressed slowly, then sat on the bed trying to think. He heard steps on the stairs. Sure it was Marilyn, he jumped from the bed and walked to the door, hoping to be moving, to appear to have direction when he met her. He stepped into the hall with his head down. The figure near the top of the stairs froze. Louise held a book in one hand, the other clutched her skirt. She looked like a schoolgirl caught in the hall without a pass.

Handle looked past her. The stairs and room below were empty. She crossed her arms in front of her chest and smiled weakly. He wanted to grab her by the shoulders and shake her but knew immediately that was dishonest. He nodded at her and hurried down the stairs.

Handle sat in the porch swing with his head tilted back and his eyes closed. The sun on his face felt good and gave him an excuse to be still. For the whole of the morning he'd tried to control the gnawing at his stomach that made him feel like a criminal. Then, lying in the sun, pretending to relax, it occurred to him that he *was* a criminal. He thought of all the punks he'd arrested who had said it seemed right at the time.

"Handle."

He recognized Marvin's deep voice but didn't want to open his eyes. "Yes," he said.

"Taking the women shopping. Might have a couple of beers if you're interested."

"Think I'll stay here."

Marvin laughed. "I dreamed about alligators last night." He laughed again. "I was raising them like cows."

Handle offered a smile and opened his eyes, shading them

from the sun with his hand. Marvin and Annalee stood just in front of him, their backs to the sun, two dark shapes connected like an amoeba in the last stages of splitting. Handle realized they were holding hands. They looked somehow comic and he laughed.

They smiled back at him, then turned and walked to their car. Handle watched them walk. The screen door opened and his wife stepped onto the porch. "You want some magazines or anything, Wayne?"

Handle looked at her for a long time before he answered by shaking his head. She smiled at him, then hurried to catch up with her parents. He watched her go, feeling she might be gone a long time. He closed his eyes and listened to the car as it drove away. He took a deep breath and tried to relax.

He decided not to think about Marilyn or Louise or anything. Wind pushed through the leaves and birds played out a tune he could almost imagine as a saxophone solo. He tried to picture himself as a teacher in a crowded classroom. But the screen door opened and the swing swayed with the weight of another. He kept his eyes closed.

Louise's voice came out of his darkness. "We should talk, Handle."

He nodded but kept his eyes closed. "I feel terrible."

"I know."

"Every time I see Marilyn, I think I'm going to cry," he said. It wasn't exactly true, but the truth was worse.

"Maybe you just need to cry."

Her voice sounded thick and low, then he heard vibration in her breathing and knew she'd begun to cry. Until his eyes became accustomed to the light, she was a blur of color. But her shape settled, and he saw her clearly: a woman, eyes red from crying, arms folded across her chest to stop herself from shaking. He saw her separate from his vision of her, as a person absolutely apart from him. A new part of her was naked, and Handle might have recognized the same in himself, but he was unable to resist touching her.

Louise shrugged his arms off her. "Someone could see," she said.

Handle looked out over the empty fields and still trees, then followed Louise inside. "It seemed right," he said when they reached the living room.

She turned and pressed her hands against his chest. They sat on the couch and held one another. Handle tried to make sense of what he felt. He closed his eyes and thought of his wife and how afraid he was of losing her. Already, he knew, he had created a distance between them. Then he thought of arriving with Marilyn at the farm, how she had burst into Louise's arms. He began to cry, knowing how much Louise had lost as well. He held her tighter, feeling closer to her than ever because of the loss they shared.

When they quit crying, Handle found he could not let her go. His arms felt solid, like cement. He knew he had to let go, but he couldn't move. His heart pounded so vigorously that he recognized it as a muscle working inside him. He kissed her. She began crying again but kissed him back. Every time he lifted a hand, it returned to her. He could pull back, but he could not pull away.

He followed Louise up the stairs to her room, where they made love again, without the clarity of emotion or the genuine belief in its honesty they'd had the night before but with the sincerest of necessity. While they made love, they listened for sounds of the car returning. They hurried, wondering how they had kept from worrying about being caught the night before. They dressed quickly afterward.

"We can never let this happen again," Louise said.

Handle had his hand on the door. "I know," he said.

They left the room separately without kissing or saying good-bye.

Handle could not stay in the house with Louise. He walked through the long, straight rows of corn quickly, directly to the woods and into the thick brush that bordered the fields.

High weeds licked the insides of his legs. The woods were dense and quiet, the trees still. Sunlight through the trees speckled the ground with moving patterns, like an active disease magnified to become visible. He walked quickly, head down, leading with his arms like a swimmer, through the woods. Louise and Marilyn played here as children, he thought as he ducked under a low limb and pushed himself through a narrow space between two trees. He was flooded with smells, the sharp green smell of the trees with new leaves, the dusty odor of bark, the mildly bitter smell of certain weeds when they broke under his step. The boy in the bar, his blank brown face, flashed in his vision, as if the boy were behind a tree watching him. Handle ignored the image and kept walking. A fallen trunk blocked his way, lying at a diagonal between trees, its white guts open, soft and spongy from rain and decay. Handle carefully placed his foot in a white pocket and lifted himself over. He pushed on, breathing heavily, his heart thudding against his chest. He lifted a thin limb and stepped under it into a narrow path. Turning immediately, he followed the path, increasing his speed. The path widened and he began to run, hands flailing at limbs and leaves. It struck him how much this was like his dream, how the path seemed like an alley, but he didn't slow down to think. His heart labored again like a muscle. The splotches of sunlight became larger. Then the forest opened up. The trees fell away. He'd reached the hollow.

His lungs aching, the muscles in his legs twitching, Handle stood erect and looked over the hollow. Milkweed and morning glories rimmed the clearing, muddled with tall grass and jimsonweed. In the middle, about fifteen yards from him, a clump of cattails grew out of the high grass. Handle leaned against a tree to catch his breath. This had been their secret place, he thought. He tried to picture them as little girls in short ruffled dresses and corn rows. His mind wouldn't cooperate, giving instead himself as a little boy with his father, not in the country but in the city, a sidewalk. A policeman tells his father that colored men do not look directly at white women and that anyone his age shouldn't have to be told. His father's face, blank and brown, his head nodding, as he assures the policeman that he wasn't doing anything and he certainly won't do it again. Handle walked into the weeds and high grass to the center. Water sloshed against his shoes and he smelled the acrid, stagnant pool of shallow water at the heart of the hollow.

As he stood among the cattails, he heard his father's voice calling someone a coal black son of a bitch. The sound of his father's voice stopped Handle, fixed him among the cattails, stationary as a tree stump. Was it that simple? Handle felt he'd just remembered a secret, as pictures of his father flashed relentlessly in his mind—his father proud his skin was lighter than his brother-in-law's, his father nodding politely to the policeman, then cursing about some niggers making it hard on the rest. Handle grabbed a handful of cattails and broke off their heads. He dropped all but one, threw it, and watched it spin like a propeller. He closed his eyes and there in his personal darkness were Louise and Marilyn.

He walked back to the edge of the hollow, but he couldn't find the path. He circled the clearing, but he'd become disoriented and had no idea which way to turn. He circled the hollow again in the opposite direction, but it did no good. Already, clouds thickened the sky. Finally, he just set out into the woods.

The randomness of the trees, the irregular angles of the branches, oppressed him. He hesitated under a thorn tree, wanting to make some kind of sense of his direction, wishing he could create a reasonable order. But the woods relinquished none of their confusion. Handle decided to simplify the world. He would think of Marilyn. He would concentrate solely on his wife and wander the woods with her image, casting out the others. He decided his love for her would prevail.

With this resolution, he began walking again. He pushed through the dense woods for over an hour before he found the trail, and with each step he pledged his love for Marilyn, Marilyn, Marilyn. By the time he emerged from the woods, he felt renewed, confident his love for his wife would defeat the darkness that threatened them.

Handle insisted that he and Marilyn prepare supper. Marvin had bought a country ham while he'd been in town. They began by slicing the ham into thick steaks. Then Marilyn tore off leaves of lettuce while Handle cut tomatoes into crescents. He found himself full of enthusiasm for the work and for his wife, kissing her on the cheek or the back of the neck after each detail of the meal was completed.

Marilyn had set out several potatoes. Handle rummaged through the silverware drawer for a potato peeler, then began peeling them, working very quickly.

Marilyn laughed. "Those were going to be baked potatoes."

Handle smiled and shrugged. "How about mashed potatoes?" She just laughed again, so he began peeling them once more. The peeling went quickly. He chopped them into smaller pieces to boil. Handle liked the appearance of the pieces of potatoes with cut edges and straight sides. He chopped them rapidly and tossed them into a pan, working with so much concentration and enthusiasm that Marilyn began to laugh. He smiled at her, then laughed himself, pressing the pan of chopped potatoes into his side. That they were together, doing something and laughing over it, delighted him and he laughed harder. He laughed until he had tears in his eyes and still laughed. He dropped the pan of potatoes and doubled over laughing. He sank to the floor and sat flat, back against a cupboard, legs straight out in front of him, and laughed. He laughed until Marilyn began to cry. He could see she was crying, but he couldn't stop laughing until she held him so tightly against her chest that she suffocated the laughter.

"You're scaring me, Wayne," she whispered. They helped each other up the stairs to bed, where they lay holding one another until Handle fell asleep.

By suppertime, rain fell like strands of hair perfectly combed. Annalee and Louise finished preparing the meal Handle and Marilyn had abandoned. They set the table, then Annalee took the dishes away and set the table again with her best china, a blue willow design passed down to her from Marvin's mother. Since Handle and Marilyn still had not come down to eat, Annalee decided to bathe and change clothes. She chose a yellow summer dress with a large ruffled collar. The dress was a gift from Marvin. She'd worn it only once, the day he'd given it to her, more than a year ago. Designed for a younger woman, the dress made Annalee look old and lean. Marvin always bought her clothes meant for younger women, due not so much to his incomprehension of fashion, although he knew nothing about it, but to his blindness to his wife's aging. Annalee knew the dress was unattractive on her and incongruent with the rainy weather, but she wanted to wear something cheerful.

Marvin sat at the head of the table. Annalee and Louise sat to his right, Handle and Marilyn to his left. He lay ham steaks on each of the plates passed to him, smelling each one and licking his lips. He still wore the overalls and work shirt he'd worn into town. Having carefully cultivated the image of a country farmer, Marvin always wore overalls when he went into town. Everyone knew he leased out his farmland, and his spotless, pressed overalls would fool no one who didn't know, but he enjoyed the masquerade and his friends played along willingly.

Louise hadn't bathed or changed clothes. The heat of the kitchen combined with the general humidity caused her white blouse to stick and wrinkle against her skin. A gravy stain ran from her first button across her heart and disappeared under her arm. Her hair, greasy with sweat, formed wet arrows across her forehead. It matted flat on one side of her head and puffed out on the other, giving her head a lop-sidedness associated with anger, with defiant carelessness. Her face had the flat, dissatisfied look of a child being punished.

As Marvin passed out the ham steaks, he told Handle about his dream of raising alligators. "Milking them was the worst," he said. "They're set so close to the ground."

Afraid to laugh after his laughing fit, Handle smiled and nodded. He kept his eyes on Marvin serving the ham or on Annalee, garish as a sunflower in her yellow dress. He didn't want to see Louise or Marilyn. Sitting at the table with both of them overtaxed his circuits. But as he accepted his plate from Marvin, he couldn't help looking at Louise. She appeared hag-gard and angry. Marvin still looked at him, and Handle felt ob-ligated to say something. He didn't want the supper to be one of those long, silent meals where people eat slowly and chew quietly. He had hoped they would talk around him. Now he had to offer something. His collar felt tight around his throat, although his shirt was unbuttoned almost halfway down his chest. "I was thinking about Amy Hansen," he offered, unsure where the words had come from.

Marilyn placed her hand over his and gently squeezed. She smiled at him. Her hand was unusually warm.

"She was your neighbor, wasn't she?" Annalee asked, a question she and everyone at the table knew the answer to.

Handle didn't know what to say. Words were too treach-erous. He shook his head. "What ever happened to her?" he said faintly. It was understood that the question was not to be answered.

He suddenly remembered a little boy who'd killed his brother during an argument. He remembered the boy sitting in the back of the patrol car while they waited for the juve-nile officers. The boy kept asking about his brother, "What's going to happen to him now?" Handle shook his head as if to shake the memory out. As quickly as it left, his father entered, on the sidewalk, hearing the white cop tell him colored men did not look directly at white women. Self-hatred washed over him for a moment, a sensation he recognized but had never before named, a legacy from his father.

Annalee had begun telling a story about a student she'd had the last year she taught, a little boy, half the size of his classmates, who gave her a poem the last day of classes. She had committed the poem to memory:

> Boys have bubbles when they talk too fast
> Girls scrape their knees worse for dresses
> Dogs eat shoes in the closet
> Teachers give everything names.

Handle filled with sadness. It became obvious to him that his life had taken a wrong turn, that he should have been a teacher. It struck him that Louise looked like a troubled child. Then he realized why she looked so bad. She'd made herself unattractive so he would have less trouble ignoring her. The realization came so suddenly he gasped for air and stared at her, knowing her matted hair and dirty shirt were emblems of love. She looked back at him and he could believe the space between them was illuminated by a field of intense yellow light. By the time she looked down, Handle felt panicky, sure they'd given themselves away. But Marilyn ate undisturbed and Marvin drank milk. Annalee's face, however, was vacant with fear and recognition.

"The rain seems so odd to me," Marilyn said, looking up from her plate. "I guess because it had been so clear in New York." She picked up her napkin and wiped the sweat from Handle's forehead. "It's so humid," she said.

No one picked up the conversation. Annalee just stared straight ahead. Handle could no longer look at her. He couldn't look at Louise, her love for him disfiguring her. He couldn't look at his wife, caring for him while she sat directly across from his lover, her sister. He looked at Marvin but had to turn away from him, so oblivious to the destruction going on around him. He looked down at his plate and realized he hadn't eaten a bite.

"I was just thinking about old Hoot," Marvin said. "Blind as a stump from eating those inky cap mushrooms. Used to chew a whole mouthful up at once." He looked at Annalee. She wasn't listening. "Annalee still claims he was just too old to see, but I know better."

"Remember when he sniffed Reverend Lee's leg, then peed on him right in the living room?" Marilyn laughed as she spoke.

Handle knew how this story was told. Annalee was ignoring her parts.

"He shit in my bed," Louise said flatly, without looking up.

Annalee turned and stared at Louise as if she'd spoken in a foreign language.

"Would have died as a pup but I ran out in the freezing cold after he'd been attacked by whatever bird it was had hatched him in the first place," Marvin chewed ham as he spoke.

Annalee was supposed to say there wasn't any such bird, so Marilyn could talk about the perfect white ground and the little dog, head up in the snow, steam rising from his exposed intestines, the snow next to him soiled by blood and shit. But Annalee wasn't speaking. She stared at Louise and Louise stared back now. Finally Louise spoke, still looking at her mother. "Mama saved the dog. She took him to the vet."

"You women always stick together," Marvin looked at Handle. "We never get credit for a thing in this household. Fact is, I practically gave the dog mouth to mouth."

"But Mama got his sight back," Marilyn said.

They looked at Annalee again. She finally turned away from Louise and back to her plate. "The dog's been dead for years," she said.

Handle wanted her to finish the story. She was supposed to tell about the bacon grease, making the path for the dog, so

Marilyn could say "to the old barn where he liked to pee," and Louise could say "to the purple magnolia where the grass was thick and soft where he liked to shit," then Marvin would jump in saying how he'd found the dog in the branches, *in the branches*, and Annalee would say that was no reason to bury him there and kill the tree. Handle could hear it all in his mind, the way it was supposed to go. "Just goes to show," Marvin would say, "that all living things are joined one way or another, everything touches everything else." Annalee would scoff, say she'd probably cut the taproot while digging the grave. But the story had been killed and hovered over them.

Louise had begun to cry silently, catching the tears with her fingers before the even left her eyes. Handle could not bear to be at the table any longer. "Excuse me," he said, but he wasn't sure he said it loud enough for anyone to hear.

He stepped into the hall, thinking he would wash his face in the bathroom sink and compose himself. He opened the door and stepped into the room quickly, closing the door behind him. The room was pitch dark. He felt for the wall switch but couldn't find it. He slapped the wall high and low, but the light switch was gone. He felt the other side. The wall was gone, the room had changed. He stepped forward. Something landed on his face. He ducked, swatted at it, but when he stood again it was back on his face. He grabbed it, a string. Pulling it, the room lit—the walk-in closet. He had turned the wrong way. He pulled the light cord again, stepped out of the closet, and crossed the hall into the bathroom.

Handle and Marilyn went to bed shortly after supper, but Handle couldn't sleep. He lay next to his wife in the dark and began to shiver as if with a fever. He sat up in bed with his back to his wife.

"Wayne."

He looked over his shoulder at her.

"Talk with me, Wayne." She switched on the light next to the bed.

"I love you," Handle said, still with his back to her. "You've got to believe that."

She placed her hand on his back. "You're just confused."

He could only stare at her.

"When we get back to New York, if you can't go back to work, then we'll find something else. Sometimes people get trapped into doing things they don't believe, and they don't even realize they're trapped. You realize it, Wayne, that's why it's so hard for you." She put an arm around him and pressed her face against his back. "Now that you've realized what's happened, it may be easier to deal with."

Handle lay back beside her in the bed. He needed to be in their bedroom. This room was too clean, too large. He needed the dark wood dresser they'd found together and began refinishing and never finished, the closet so stuffed with clothes the door was always open. He needed the clutter of married life to remind him who he was.

"It's just the police," Marilyn said. "You meet so many desperate people." She took his chin, turned him to face her. "You're not racist, Wayne. You know you love me. How could you love me if you were racist? How could you love yourself?" She kissed his forehead. "You love me, you just told me so. And you love Mama and Daddy. You love . . . ."

Handle cupped his palm over her mouth to stop her. He pulled her close and kissed her. She turned out the light and they kissed once more.

It was still dark. Handle had slept twice during the night, once for almost an hour. He let his eyes adjust to the darkness and looked at the shape his wife made in the bed as he slipped on his pants.

He walked down the stairs quietly, carefully, and stepped into the living room. Louise was in the corner. She had no book. There was no light. The comforter was wrapped tightly around her. When she saw him, she began shaking her head. She covered her face with her hands.

"I've been here all night," she whispered. "I was hoping you wouldn't come."

She stood. They held each other, afraid to talk. She led him out of the living room into the hall. She opened the door to the walk-in closet and spread the comforter. With the door closed, the closet was absolutely dark. They positioned themselves carefully away from the walls, which might creak if pressed against. They made love, controlling their breathing as much as they could, pausing if they heard a noise. When they finished, they kissed once, but neither could say that what they'd done was right or that it was over or that there was any escape.

Flipflops

"I know a joke," I say.

Alice is next to me, lying on a canvas recliner in a stylish striped bathing suit, legs crossed, beads of sweat sliding across her oiled skin. Her sunglasses, perfect brown eggs, rest on the bridge of her nose at the proper angle, her lips part to the precise degree of desire. Even her feet, busy against one another, point to the sand like the feet of a dancer suspended in flight. The beach is crowded, people like us, down from the States for the long Thanksgiving weekend, escaping the cold, maybe in love. Alice and I have never been together before, never made love. We broke off relationships to come here, believing we needed distance to satisfy longing.

She lowers her sunglasses, smiles behind the perfect eggs. Her face is handsome, solid, visibly relieved that I have something to say. The boldness of our trip has made us shy, smiling at our silences in the plane, playing with our poor Spanish in the taxi, changing clothes separately in our room. The closest connection we've made so far was agreeing on identical purple flipflops in the garish hotel shop.

"There was a man with three arms," I say.

She turns on her side to face me. Arms and legs cross. "Is this a penis joke?"

"No, that's three legs." A man in long pants and shoes walks through the sand carrying a box of jewelry, opals and obsidian, but I wave him off. Children in jagged brown cutoffs play tag with the advancing and receding water. Middle-aged women sit in the shallows, cupping water to their shoulders, talking and staring back at the beach with the flat expressions of concealed boredom. Beyond them, two men challenge one another to swim farther, waving and laughing. "The man with three arms is lonely, so he goes to a fortune-teller."

"Here?"

"Not Mexico." I shake my head, think. "Virginia, small town, has a name like a woman's name, like Rhonda. Rhonda, Virginia. The fortune-teller's name is May."

Alice laughs. "Her last name is Bee, right? May Bee, the fortune-teller."

"No, let me tell this or it'll take all day."

"I need the details."

The sun is high. An old couple, white as fence posts, hold hands and wade into the water up to their knees, thighs, hips. One young woman, her belly hanging over her sulfur yellow bikini bottom, picks her way carefully through a patch of sharp rocks on the beach. The two men dare each other out farther.

"Her last name is Josephine. May Josephine, fortune-teller. So the man with three arms . . ."

"What's his . . ."

"Ted. Ted Tommy. So Ted goes to May."

"Everyone has two first names." She lifts a knee, runs her foot along her reclining calf, toes pointed, still the feet of a dancer. The bell-shaped woman draws near, flabby-chested, hair pooched up on one side and streaked with sand.

"He asks if he will ever find a woman who'll love him despite his third arm. She looks at her cards and says yes, there's that possibility. He gets very excited and asks, 'When? How do I meet her?' And so on. The fortune-teller tells him to come back in three weeks."

Alice shakes her head. "This isn't going to be one of those long jokes that's only funny because it takes so long to get so little?"

"No, that's life. This is a joke." The sulfur bikini walks past again, returning to the water, the stem of a beachball in her mouth. The ball droops over her chin, the same partially inflated oblong of her breasts. Beyond her, one wave erases the next like a succession of thoughts. "So Ted goes around for three weeks very excited."

"What's he do?"

The sulfur bikini runs a finger around her waistband, dredging an inch of sand. The two swimmers are all arms and backs. "He's a . . . let me think." Alice and I met at work, the university. She's a graduate student in biology and I work in the office.

"A typist," she says.

"No, a milkist. A milker. He milks cows."

"They use machines for that."

"Not when there's a man with three arms."

She shakes her head and laughs, a concession, the same gesture she made when I told her I wanted to see her, have lunch, dinner, a movie, leave our lovers. I had been seeing a computer programmer who wrote poetry, wore used clothes, and shredded the three shirts I left in her closet. Alice had been dating an optometrist with perfect vision and a gap between his front teeth.

"By day he milks, by night he frets." I touch her arm, hot—we're burning up out here. Alice looks at my hand on her arm with a curious stare, as if a bird had lighted there. "Three weeks finally pass and he goes back. She lays out the cards and says he'll meet her in precisely three more weeks if all goes well."

"Sounds like a scam."

"He asks what he needs to do. She says to brush his hair, teeth, and shoes three times a day, using a different hand for each chore but the same brush."

"This is getting really silly." She laces her fingers across her chest. Alice doesn't like nonsense.

A beach waiter arrives with two sweating beers I ordered an hour ago. Alice hands me my wallet from her purse. I give the waiter a wad of pesos. He's chunky, in a long green wedding shirt that makes him look like a huge papaya. He hands most of the wad back to me, leaves before I can calculate a tip. "So Ted's shaken." I hand the wallet back to Alice. I drink. She drinks. "But he does it, brushes his hair with his right hand, his teeth with his left hand, and his shoes with his middle hand."

"Middle hand? Where does this third arm grow from?"

"His chest, right over his heart." When I say this, her face flattens slightly. We drink again. I feel there's something I want to ask her, something to do with us, but I don't know what it is, and there's the joke to finish. "So he brushes each three times a day, using his toothbrush since that's the only one that would fit in his mouth." I wait for a smile, but she doesn't so I hurry it up. "Three weeks pass. On the final day he's milking as usual and the daughter of the dairy farmer comes to him and says, 'I've been noticing you. Why do you use the same brush on your hair, teeth, and shoes?' He smiles at her. She's very pretty."

"All women in jokes are. Or very ugly. Mark used to tell jokes about ugly women. It bothered me." She shades her eyes with her hand, a black shadow slashes her face. Mark is the optometrist. He used to wait for her in the biology office, hands in his pockets, slouched against a wall, gap-toothed smile. I panic for an instant, thinking he may have told me this joke, but I decide not. It's a joke I grew up with. I just haven't told it in a while.

"He explains about the fortune-teller and that this is the day the woman who could love him should come and, sure enough, the farmer's daughter falls in love with him."

Suddenly the sulfur bikini drops her beach ball and stands bolt upright, her back to us. The women in the shallows stand and face the ocean. One of the boys in jagged brown cutoffs points. I look out over the water.

"So?" Alice asks.

"So," I shade my eyes but see nothing. "So, it just goes to show." The man with the jewelry is beside us again but ignoring us, staring out at the Pacific. "A brush in the hand," I say. "No, a brush in each hand. A third brush. Wait a minute." The man with the jewelry begins running, kicking sand against my chest. "A brush in the hand is worth a third in the chest."

"That's not it," Alice says. She sits up straight, stares at the people lining the water's edge.

"Wait," I say, looking at the people but trying to remember the punch line. "Two in the brush is worth a third in the hand. Something like that." I want to say it's the telling that matters, but she's already standing.

"Something's going on out there," she says.

I stand, look out beyond the crowd. The swimmers have gone too far. One is struggling in, the other just a waving arm, a dark head. "He's drowning," I say and begin running toward the water, across the cutting rocks, pushing between the old couple, white as fence posts. One, two, three high steps into the water, then dive beneath a surging wave, pull and kick to the surface, then it's automatic. I'm a swimmer. Fifty laps every morning at the university pool. But this water's thick, the waves insistent. Swing, pull, kick, and twist.

Well into the ocean, I do a pop-up to locate them. One brown man is within twenty yards to my right. Duck, swing, pull, kick, twist. The water is cold. I needed to stretch before I began swimming, warm up. The swimmer is there, T-shirt transparent with water. He's treading hard, slaps the water, shakes his head, says something unintelligible, points farther out. I can see his buddy spitting water, thrashing, another thirty yards, maybe more.

Swing, pull. The cold settles in my muscles. They become brittle. Kick, twist, swing. A wave slaps against my face and head. Another pop-up. Nothing. The ocean rising and falling. A hand. Twenty yards farther still. Swing, pull. I have to think it through, tell my legs to kick, kick, kick. My arms pull in next to my chest. I argue with my arms. Swing, kick, pull. I've messed up the order, working against myself. I stop, tread, my knees jerk up to my chest. The man is gone. I shiver in the water, try one dive, but I can see nothing in the murky Pacific, feel nothing but the cold, the stinging red of my eyes, the painful arguments of my muscles. I turn back.

I backstroke. The sun finds slightly more of me. Backstroking, returning to shore, my body in agreement, I take a deep breath. The man has drowned or is drowning. I backstroke. The sky is mimeo blue.

The first step in shallow water, my knees buckle, but I right myself, wait for a wave to push my thighs forward. Alice is at the water's edge, arms crossed, hands on her shoulders, striped suit, brown eggs. "I couldn't reach him," I say, but too softly, an asthmatic cough.

She runs to me, ties her arms around me. Waves rush our calves. "You're cold," she says.

As she says it, I begin to shiver. Her hands flatten against my back, move up and down in arcs. The first swimmer made it back to shore. He lies on his back in the sand. A crowd, ridiculous in beach clothes that barely cover their bodies, has gathered around him. "Bodies should be covered," I say.

"He's alive," Alice says.

"No, the others." I point at the garish crowd. We walk back toward our beach chairs. Alice is wearing her flipflops, but the rocks tear at my feet. I stop. "Would you grab my flip-flops?" I ask her.

She nods, hurries across the patch of rocks and stretch of sand to our chairs. Her body twists and curves perfectly, but her stylish striped suit seems ridiculous too. She reaches the chairs, begins circling, head down. I left the flipflops by my chair, but Alice doesn't see them. I take another step. These are not rocks, I think, these are teeth.

"I can't seem to find them," she says when I finally reach the chairs. I search with her, but they're gone.

"Check your purse," I say, but nothing else is missing.

The crowd is helping the surviving swimmer walk to the hotel. His arms, flabby from fatigue, are around the shoulders of two large men. His wet T-shirt droops from his shoulders like age. Alice and I watch the group as they pass. The swimmer looks directly at me but either doesn't recognize me or chooses not to acknowledge me. The others seem to follow his example, saying nothing.

I look over their feet. Most are barefoot, some in leather thongs, a few flipflops. I scrutinize the flipflops—oranges, grays, reds, greens, one purple pair—a woman, skinny, short dark hair, a black bathing suit stretched over her body like a frown. She trudges through the sand in the rear of the crowd. Her flipflops are much too large for her feet. They're mine.

I grab Alice's shoulder, point. "My flipflops." I hurry over to the crowd, pulling Alice along. "Pardon me," I say loudly.

The crowd looks me over, even the men helping the swimmer. "Pardon me." I approach the skinny woman. "Those are my flipflops," I say.

She looks straight ahead as if she can't hear.

I grab her arm. "My flipflops," I say and point. *"Mis zapatos."*

She jerks her head in my direction. "I speak English," she says, looks away, begins walking again with the group.

"I want my flipflops."

"These are not yours." She still doesn't look at me.

Two dark men in matching bathing suits and life jackets carrying a rowboat above their heads run past us to the water. Alice puts her hands on my waist, pulls me toward her. "Forget it," she whispers.

"I want my flipflops," I say and grab the woman's arm again, jerk her around to face me.

The skinny woman glares at me, then kicks off the flipflops. One bounces off my shin; the other slaps Alice in the pelvis.

For Thanksgiving dinner, we order steaks, rare. The restaurant in the hotel overlooks the ocean, which, at dusk, is as gray as the sky. Muzak cowboy songs are playing—"Back in the Saddle Again," "Tumbling Tumbleweeds," others I don't recognize. At least one person at each of the tables near us has a decapitated pineapple with a straw growing out of it, so when Alice orders Scotch and water, I'm relieved. In a new blue blouse and white skirt, she looks as fresh as new sheets. Changing out of beach clothes has made us familiar again. All afternoon we avoided talking about the drowning by avoiding talking. I slept while she read, then stared at the ocean, the rowboat bobbing in the distance, while she took a nap. Still we're hardly talking, but the silence is more comfortable.

When I first met Alice, she had a cold, sniffling into a tissue while she explained her interest in desert biology, how life in the desert persevered against the odds. Her nose was red, eyes watery. Later I told her she was more beautiful with a cold, that hers was the kind of face that needed flaws. It's her sunburned nose that reminds me, and I begin to wonder if I'll like her best in the mornings before coffee and makeup, and that makes me wonder if there will be mornings. The steaks arrive, overcooked, with refried beans, rice, and green peas.

"I don't think I've ever had steak for Thanksgiving," Alice offers. She slices away a triangle of meat.

"One Thanksgiving, when I was an undergrad," I say, "I ate moldy cottage cheese and day-old bagels." It's a lie, but it fills the space between us.

"I remember one Christmas." She touches the cloth napkin to her lips. "The turkey hadn't thawed. My mother was sick and Father was trying to do everything. He was an awful cook but he had beautiful eyes, like yours, like . . . I want to say like spearmint, but that's a flavor." She gently prods my hand with her finger. "We ate pimento cheese sandwiches and Sara Lee pound cake."

We laugh, hold hands for a moment, then eat. The steak is more tender than it looks but, for some reason, hard to swallow. I fill up on beans and rice. Several tables away, the old couple from the beach stand and walk toward the exit. They see me watching and come to our table. The woman hangs back, smiling sadly and nodding, holding a small white purse tight against her abdomen. The man, overdressed in a white shirt and bow tie, puts a hand on my shoulder. He shakes his head, frowns, shrugs. "The ocean," he says, as if in explanation.

I nod and they leave.

"You look good in water," Alice says, her face intent, as if she's trying to remember something. "The way you just started running . . ." She's looking past me so intensely I almost turn, but she drops her gaze to her plate. "He was a long way out."

I watch her slice her steak. "I was on the swim team in high school," I tell her. "Once I swam two hundred laps for some charity. Multiple Sclerosis, I think."

"I mowed lawns for March of Dimes." She whirls her fork in a tight circle next to her face. "Baked brownies for Muscular Dystrophy. Washed cars for Battered Wives."

"Get along Little Dogies" begins playing in the background. I smile at her, stir my beans, rice, and peas together. "The credit union donated a dollar for every lap I swam. My shoulders ached for a month."

She reaches across the table, stops me from stirring. "I was scared while you were out there." She looks out the window at the ocean. "I was afraid you might drown, then—this is awful—I tried to think how I'd explain being here with you."

"Did you come up with something?"

She nods. "Research." She giggles, and I remember that her laughter is one of the things that attracted me. "Oh, I would have told the truth, but it sounds so tragic. I hate people feeling sorry for me."

"So what is the truth?" I lean closer to her. "Why *are* you here?"

She smiles, looks at her lap, then the ocean. "Look," she says, "your friends."

The old couple, holding hands, stand near the water's edge. They're both pointing. Three men appear and, behind them, others I can't make out. The men roll up their pants, begin wading in, then spread apart, circling.

"What are they doing?" I ask.

Alice shakes her head, shrugs.

The tallest man gestures to the others. They bend over, lift a body out of the shallow water. The tall one has the hands, the others a foot each. I feel my body pull back.

"This is awful," Alice says. I don't know whether she means the scene outside or us. I turn to face her. She could be the swimmer's widow, so dark is her face. I turn back. The real widow has run barefoot across the sharp rocks to the body. Her hands go from the tangle of her short hair to her husband's bloated body. She wraps her arms around his trunk, but just as quickly she jumps back, away from the body. She drops to her knees, wipes at her arms where they touched him. The three men carry the body away.

Alice touches my arm. I jump. "What?"

"That's her, isn't it?" she says.

"Who?"

"The one who took your flipflops."

I stand, fork and napkin fall. I press my face against the window.

"That's her, isn't it?" Alice says.

I hood my eyes with my hands to stop the glare of the restaurant lights. "It can't be," I say.

"That's her," Alice says. "That's her."

The woman takes a handful of sand, rubs her arms with it.

"No," I say. "That's not her."

Alice tugs at my shirt. I sit back at the table, and we eat our Thanksgiving steaks.

Finally in bed together, I can do nothing, my penis soft and small as a child's. We hold each other. I run my hands down the soft curve of her back again and again. The walls in this room, I realize, are yellow, most yellow near the night lamp, muted by the dark in the corners. There is a painting of a brown boy in a ridiculously large sombrero standing next to a smiling mule. On the dresser, our clothes make happy shapes, like party favors.

"You know any more jokes?" Alice whispers.

Our clothes on the dresser, I think, this room. But I don't say that. I shake my head.

"What about the other? Do you remember the punch line?"

I try to remember. When I can't, I try to reconstruct it.

"A bird in the hand is worth two in the bush. Third would be bird," I say.

"Brush would be bush," she says.

"It doesn't go together. I got thrown off course."

Alice raises up on one elbow. "Maybe the daughter doesn't fall in love with him."

"Maybe." I nod and we become so quiet that I can hear the ocean rushing toward us and human sounds in the room next door.

"Maybe he falls in love with the fortune-teller," Alice says. "Or with his fortune."

"Or with the telling," I say and pull her close, but to get her really close would require something else, something like a third arm. I try to think what it might be.

Alice touches my cheek with her fingertips, then turns off the lamp and the room goes dark. "Do you think we did right coming here?" she asks.

"I don't know," I say, but it comes out a whisper and I lose track of my thoughts.

The Right Thing

His feet are the size of thumbs, the segments of his toes no larger than grains of rice. I slap him on the bottom the way I've heard to do. He squeaks and sucks in air, then begins to cry. His fingers bend, grasp for something. I put my little finger in his hand. He clings to it. It's enough for now. He cries for milk. But his mother's breasts are blue, streaked with grease, splattered with blood.

When I lift my hand, I'm not there at all. There's no baby but a woman, a girl, seventeen. Her nipples, no larger than dimes, point to her chin. She licks her lips in her sleep. Blue veins divide the underside of her tongue. Her hair is crossparted by sleep, blonde as matchwood. The sparse light hair on her upper lip is damp from her tongue. I wrap my hand around her thin wrist, run my index finger over the thick vein at the base of her palm, feel the simple rhythm of blood. I cling to her slender wrist.

I close my eyes and I'm in a village without a name outside of Huan Fo. I open my eyes. The girl is there. When I lift the curtain it's morning in Illinois. Her brother is in the yard with his back to the window, a can of gasoline in his hand. I close my eyes. In the village, the rhythm of strafing fades, falters, continues to fade. The knife that could cut hair off an arm without bending the follicles slits her abdomen into perfect halves. Out of her dead body, a child the color of sky. The petroleum smell of napalm coughs into the child's lungs, and the tiny body reddens against the wind of his own breath. The sound of strafing begins to increase in volume. The child is drenched in his mother's blood. His tiny hand closes around my finger. "Hagget." The voice should be Olson's, but it's not. "Hagget." I look at the child. "Hagget."

The girl is over me, eyes green as black market jade. The tiny space between her front teeth glistens with a bubble of saliva. She licks her lips. "Hagget." I nod. I hear the lawn mower out the window, coming nearer, loud and rhythmic, then the sound recedes. The odor of gasoline trails the sound.

"Hagget, you're about to break my arm." I look down at my hand around her wrist. I let go.

She kisses the base of my neck and an involuntary groan escapes my throat. Her body snakes around mine. The twist from ribs to hips exaggerates the curves, heightens the angles, giving her the illusion of womanliness while she still has the soft, taut skin that is peculiarly a girl's. She moves her knee between my legs, slowly raises it to nudge my penis and testicles. I kiss her, her tongue exploding into my mouth, and wait for the sensation of desire to crowd out drowsiness. I believe, but I know it's my imagination, that my tongue can detect the blue vein in her tongue, trace the raised canal, detect the difference in temperature of the deoxygenated blood within the vein. I picture it as a cold string running directly to her heart, and suddenly the weight settles in my penis and in my testicles, hundred-watt bulbs are switched on.

"I love you, Hagget," she says. "I love you, Hagget." We come together comfortably, effortlessly. "I love you, Hagget. I love you." We come together at the perfect pitch and sex becomes its own animal, encompassing both of us, startling us again with the same surprise. "I love you, Hagget." Even the lawn mower's hum, rising as it nears the window again, the spit of the motor, becomes part of our sex, vibrating through us. I picture the whip of the blade. "I love you, Hagget," she says.

The lawn is mowed. The sound of the shower is the same sound as Spam frying in a skillet. During the summer months, the girl sometimes showers three or four times a day. She takes long showers. I can taste burnt Spam, the charred taste finding the corners of my mouth, the static crunch of blackened meat. Are there gnats in this room? There are no gnats in this room. The first time Olson found a leech on his leg, he threw up. They leave scars, some of them. In a pinch you can eat them. That's what they told us. You can eat leeches:

boiled, fried maybe. "Broasted," Olson had said. "I only eat leeches broasted." And human flesh, when it burns, smells familiar. It's just like something I've smelled before, but I could never quite put my finger on it.

The radio is on the fritz. I hear Olson pound it with his fist. I think I see sparks, but I'm not sure. My eyes could just be making colors in the dark. The rain has stopped, but the darkness is absolute. I hear Olson hit the radio again, smell burning rubber, then a smell like a car overheating, no—like hair burning. "I can't see a thing," I say. "Jesus Christ, I can't see my hands. I can't see my fucking hands."

"Shut up," Olson says, and I hear the radio splash into the shallow water of the rice paddy. Water rises and falls against my legs, once, twice, ruffles against me, then is still.

"How far away are you?" I ask.

"I don't know," Olson says. "How far away are you?"

"I don't know," I say. "You sound like you're near."

"How loud are you talking? Are you talking loud?"

"I don't know. I don't think I'm talking loud. Are you talking loud?"

"Does this sound like a whisper?" he asks. "I think I'm whispering."

"I'm going to move my hands around," I say. "I'm going to see if you're real near. You might be near." I'm on my back, M-16 in my left hand, butt end in the water. My right hand is against my chest. I push against my ribs, move down my side to the water. My fingers reach the bottom, press against the cool mud. Water runs up my sleeve. I move my hand away from my body, patting the ground, which slopes upward to the grassy ridge of the paddy. Out of the water, blades of grass, pebbles, a rock, no, a limb, no—

"My boot," Olson says. "Is that your hand on my boot?"

"I don't know. It could be a boot. I'm going to move it, all right?"

"All right."

I shake it and it rolls into the water. My fingers jump back and grope my face. The M-16 falls against my knee and splashes into the water. "Was that your boot? Was that your boot?"

"I don't know," he says. "I can't feel anything."

"Find your feet," I say. "Hurry, find your feet."

"All right. Wait. Got them."

"You got them? Both of them?"

"I got them both."

"Good," I say. "That's good."

"Where do you think we are?" he asks.

I fish my rifle out of the water. "I think we're close to each other," I say.

"Hagget. I love you, Hagget."

I open my eyes and the girl is standing over me, blue towel around her. Drops of water cling to her neck and shoulders, the declivities of her collarbones. She kisses my forehead.

"You take long showers," I say.

"Is your friend coming today?" she asks. "Is he finally going to make it?" She's smiling. Wet, her hair is darker and parts in the middle.

"You're very pretty," I say, looking at the indentions of her dimpled cheeks. She is pretty, very cute, very pretty.

"Breakfast is ready." She runs a thumb over my chin, down my neck to my sternum. She giggles. "Mama bought a ham. You love ham."

"I love ham," I say.

"I love *you*," she says.

Olson was supposed to go to Mexico with me. I couldn't stay in Illinois at first. The people's faces seemed elongated, like game show contestants on a bad television. I needed a trip. I called Olson in Nebraska and he said, "Sure, sure, Mexico. I'll go." But I went alone, reassured in the north by the desert, the barrenness interrupted by the stolid saguaro, the gnarled creosote. The desert seemed complacent. Then in

Mexico City, the ride to the pyramids on the broken-down bus, jarring my teeth like a rifle, and everywhere the smell of exhaust, Mexican children selling trinkets—ceramic flutes, obsidian, bananas, mangoes, oranges.

Oranges and bananas are okay, a middle-aged woman from Wyoming tells me. "The book says they're okay. Anything with a peel." I stuff a short green banana in my khaki pocket, throw the boy a coin. He grins. Too much money. I walk quickly to lose the Wyoming woman. The stairs up the Pyramid of the Sun are steep. Halfway up I see a woman, flushed in the face, slumped on the stones, sucking air in like a shock. Beside her, her husband pats her back, adjusts the lens on his Minolta.

At the top are mostly kids, one pair of lovers nuzzling. I try to picture the sacrifice. Giving over to the sun. A woman, I think, a girl, perhaps a virgin, a child, a young man. Overhead, a 747 drones, Trans World Airlines. Below, the sharp-cut stones, steep stairs, people in clusters. I pull out the banana and peel it, staring at the next pyramid, the Pyramid of the Moon, and the aisle below, the Avenue of the Dead. I try to picture men selling dogs, pottery, but instead I'm in a village without a name, a thick-bladed knife, sharp enough to cut hair off an arm without bending the follicles, in my hand. I drop the banana and run down the stairs, always down the stairs, to the Avenue of the Dead, where hundreds of years before people gave up their lives willingly for sunlight.

The game of the week is on, Boston and the Yankees. Yaz hits one off the wall but Pinella holds him to a single. The Green Monster, Fenway Park, no score in the eighth. Where's Olson? A short drive, he said, be there by noon. My watch says 1:21. Every time we talk it's the same. He's just lost his job, but he's got prospects. We only talk on the phone. I've never seen him in this country. When I tell him Linda is seventeen, he says he wants to meet her, but his voice is unconvincing. Over the telephone, his voice sounds nasal, forced.

"This Linda have a sister?"

"No sisters," I tell him. "We could fish. The fishing's good here."

"I just love fishing," he says, but without seeing his face I can't tell whether he's serious or sarcastic. That's the trouble with phones, like talking in the dark. "How's your job?" he asks.

"Steady. There's plenty of work. I could get you on."

"I don't know construction."

"It's landscape. I do landscape."

"I don't know landscape."

"You coming this time?"

"Sure, sure. I'll be there. It's not that far. Noon at the latest."

My watch says 1:24. Yaz is caught trying to score from first on a single. He arrived before the ball, but the plate was blocked. He couldn't find home. "What the hell are they doing?" Olson wants to know.

The blades of the helicopter whip the air insistently, with purpose, landing direct blows on the membranes of my ears. The first flares lead us out of the paddies, then the strafing begins. The gunners become mechanical, no longer real people; their helmets vibrate all the thoughts out of their heads. Then again the one chopper. The fire in the village is from the supply truck our squad abandoned. When was that? Three hours ago? Five hours ago? I look at my watch. It says 1:32. I can't keep track of time in the dark.

"What the hell are they doing?" Olson asks again. The sound of the strafing answers and beneath it the sound of dying: short shrieks, mechanical barks. The plane with the gunners circles again, strafing the trees, the paddies. We duck, flatten against the ground. One chopper, a solid beam of light supports it. Another pass, the strafing falters, then begins to fade. The beam of light evaporates and the chopper becomes just a noise, wet sheets fluttering in a stiff wind. We walk cautiously toward the burning supply truck. "The fucks," Olson says. "The dumb fucks."

I hear the doorbell and rise. Linda and her mother are shopping. Her brother is in the backyard, pruning the trees. The shears open with a sigh, close with a bark. I look at the television as I stand. The ball game is over. I don't know who won. Someone is fishing on television. The doorbell again and at the door, Olson.

"I had a flat," he says. His hair is laced with gray, jeans and shirt blue, hands moving at his hips, all his weight on one leg.

"You got gray," I say. We shake hands. "Want a beer?"

I bring the beers to the living room, where two men now fish on television. They have long poles and seem to be enjoying themselves. When they talk to one another, they whisper. We watch them and drink. Olson looks at me, then back at the television. I nod at him, but his head turns too quickly. I look back at the men fishing, up to their hips in water. The current is swift and one pulls the other through. I look back at Olson. He's looking at me, turns away, then turns back, drinks his beer. I look back at the television. A man is shaving and Olson says, "What the fuck am I doing here?"

I look at him, shake my head. "I wanted to see you."

"Why? For Christsakes, why?"

"I got no idea."

"The war?" he asks. "You want to talk war? I don't want to talk war. Fuck the war."

"I don't want to talk war either," I say.

"What else we got to talk about?" he asks.

I shake my head again. "Nothing. We got nothing but the war."

We stare at each other a while, then watch the two men fish. They catch a river bass, big as two hands. They slap one another on the back. "I get letters," Olson says. "From some of the guys."

I nod. "Anyone doing all right?"

He shrugs. "I got a picture from Truman. You remember Truman? Took a picture of all of us, most of us, one afternoon."

"Huan Fo," I say. Outside the bar, we stand with arms

around each other. Olson's hands playing with his belt, his weight on one leg. He makes faces at the camera.

"I look like a fucking grinning hyena." Olson spits out a laugh.

I can hardly stand and have to lean on Olson while Truman fiddles with the lens. Sunlight shines directly on my face and neck. Water fills the ruts in the roads, the declivities in the plankboard steps. Truman has one boot in a murky puddle.

"He send you one?"

I look at Olson. The grin is gone, long gone. "Long time ago. Don't know what I did with it."

"I hated Huan Fo. More than anyplace."

"The village," I say.

"Huh?"

"The village without a name just outside of Huan Fo."

"The fucks," Olson says. "The dumb fucks."

The burning supply truck is the only light. The flames shoot high and near them the yellow light is constant. At our feet, the ground is shadow and light, shadow and light. Across her body, shadow and light. "She the one this afternoon? At the truck?" I ask.

"She's the one," Olson says.

I bend over her. She's naked, pregnant, charred face, grease smeared across her breasts, blood splattered from her shoulders to her belly. "Her clothes burn off?"

"I don't know," Olson says.

I touch her inflated belly. "Oh, Jesus," I say. "Oh, Jesus."

"What?" he asks. "What is it?"

"I can feel it kick. The baby. I can feel it kick."

"Hagget." It should be Olson's voice. "Hagget." It is his voice. I look at him but there's no knife. He doesn't have the knife. "Hagget, you want another beer?"

He's calling from the refrigerator. I look hard at him. "A beer," I say.

He pauses, pulls two beers from the refrigerator.

"The right thing," I say. "We did the right thing."

He walks over to me, shoves the beer next to my face. I take it, open it, drink a long swallow. Olson sits again, says nothing. Outside, Linda's brother starts the chain saw to finish pruning the trees. My hands are covered with blood, but the baby sucks in air like a shock and cries. Next to the burning truck, an old woman and two small boys huddle together. The boys cry in long, forced breaths. The woman holds her head in her hands. She lifts her head, extends her arms in our direction. "The baby," Olson says. "She wants the baby." I cup the baby in my palms, hold him away from my body, and move toward the woman slowly. She takes him. I run backward to Olson, the rifle over my shoulder thuds against the back of my thigh. As I stop, the sound of strafing surfaces, becomes louder. The two boys begin running immediately. Olson and I begin to run. The woman doesn't run.

"Run," I yell at her.

"Run," Olson yells.

She doesn't run. I point my rifle at her. I shoot the ground around her feet. She doesn't run. The strafing comes nearer, gunners swinging back and forth, everything goes, everything goes. "Run, goddamn it." She won't run.

"Hagget."

I look at Olson, the beer still in his hand.

"Who is that with the chain saw?"

"Linda's brother," I tell him.

"Tell him to turn it the fuck off, will you?"

I nod, but before I can stand the chain saw stops. Silence descends, hovers, whips back any attempt at conversation. We sleep next to each other on the edge of a paddy. Olson starts to cry and that starts me crying. We hold each other. The night is absolute, but the smell of the burning truck seeps through the darkness. Our crying stops and fatigue settles in its place. Something is added to the smell of the burning truck, a familiar smell, one I can't quite put my finger on. I begin crying again.

I hear the front door open and close. Linda enters the

room, carrying a bag of groceries. She walks immediately to my chair and places a hand on my cheek. She looks at Olson. "You must be Hagget's friend. I'm Linda."

They shake hands.

"You're as pretty as Hagget told me." Olson smiles.

I run my hand from her ankle to her thigh. She's wearing running shorts and a blue T-shirt.

"Are you going to stay for supper?" she asks.

He smiles but shakes his head.

I go to bed early, try to read a play. Linda is in the shower again. When the darkness lifts, Olson fries Spam in a skillet he carries in his pack. Spam smells nothing like human flesh. It hardly smells like meat at all. He wipes the blade of the thick knife carefully with the tail of his shirt, but he cuts the shirt nonetheless. He slices the Spam into two equal pieces. I spear it with the blade of my pocketknife and eat around the edges. He puts another slice on the skillet to cook. "How much longer you think it'll last?" Olson asks me.

"How much longer will what last?"

"The war. What else?"

I shake my head. "I don't know." I try to picture the war over. "I can't picture it ever ending."

"Can't go on forever," he says.

"It can't?"

"I don't think so," he says.

"I don't know."

"I don't either."

The sizzling suddenly stops and I'm in a room in Illinois. Linda opens the bedroom door. She's wrapped in a yellow towel, which she lets fall as she closes the door and crawls into bed. "I like your friend, Hagget."

"He liked you," I say.

She smiles, rests her head on my chest. Water beads on my chest from her hair. I run my hand over her moist back. "He didn't stay very long," she says.

I nod, but her head on my chest faces the wall, she can't see me nodding. She lifts her head and looks me in the face, drops of water trailing down her forehead. "He didn't stay long."

I nod again.

"I love you, Hagget." She kisses my chin, lips, cheek. I kiss her. The doorbell rings, then three quick thuds on the door. I look at the digital clock on the nightstand. 10:36. "I'll get it," I say, nodding again. "I'll get the door."

I'm naked, my penis partially erect. I lift a terry cloth robe from the heap of clothes on the closet floor. The doorbell sounds again.

"Hurry, before it wakes Mother."

I look at her as I pull the robe around me. She's smiling, pointing at my penis. The doorbell sounds again, more thuds. I walk quickly down the hall. "Who's there?" I call from the living room.

"Hagget?"

"Olson? Is that you, Olson?"

"Hagget?" Three more thuds on the door. "Hagget?"

I open the door. Olson reaches for my arm immediately. "How's my Hagget?" He squeezes my arm, smiles. In his right hand he holds a paper sack.

"I thought you went home," I say.

He stares at my bare feet, then the robe, finally my eyes. "Domesticated, Hagget. She buy this for you?" Olson grips the robe, then releases it. He giggles and pulls a pistol out of the paper sack. He lets the sack fall and puts his fingers to his lips. "Shh." He uses the pistol to part the robe, which falls open, and pokes the barrel in my navel. "You got to keep this for me." He punctuates with a prod into my belly.

I look down at the pistol. "What happened?"

He flutters his fingers in front of his face. "Shh." He starts to giggle and the pistol brushes against my penis. "I'm a little drunk tonight, Hagget." He pokes the barrel hard into my belly, then turns it flat. I cup my hand over his. He pulls away and I'm pressing the gun against my belly.

"You shoot somebody, Olson?"

"Oh, Hagget. Goddamn you, Hagget." He's almost whisper-ing. "Goddamn you." He grabs my testicles. "Got any balls left, Hagget?"

I push his shoulder. He falls back but doesn't let go. He straightens himself, grips harder, and rolls his fingers. "You got any balls at all?"

I stick the barrel of the pistol in his ear.

He laughs out loud, then covers his mouth with both hands. "Shh," he says. "I did the right thing." He gives another half laugh, turns, walks toward the street.

"Olson."

He keeps walking.

"Olson."

He turns and faces me. "Keep it for me. Keep it all for me." He backs onto the asphalt, pivots, and trots to his car.

In the bedroom, I wrap the pistol in the robe and stuff it under my T-shirts in a drawer. Linda is already asleep, on her side, one knee bent, one leg straight. I lie next to her. Her hand pats my leg, then falls back to the bed. I put my arms around her, pull her close. Her nipple presses into the center of my palm.

Truman tries to get everyone to come outside together for a picture. "Take the fucker in here," Olson yells.

"Too dark," Truman mumbles, then says louder, "you're all in the dark."

Somebody yells for someone to turn on the lights, but they're already on. "We need sunlight," I say and stand. Olson stands also and we begin stumbling toward the door and the light beyond.

I open my eyes and I'm in Illinois darkness. The digital clock on the nightstand says 2:48. Linda sleeps on her stom-ach, sheet up to her waist, one hand tangled in her hair, the other off the edge of the bed. I sit and throw off the sheet, pull back the curtain on the dark lawn, empty street, the stark

light of the streetlamp. I let the curtain flutter closed—
shadow and light, shadow and light. I try to think about
Olson, the gun, but I remember Mexico, downtown Puerto
Vallarta, an old hotel, and on the roof a swimming pool and a
view of the ocean.

I sit with my back to the ocean, staring at the swimmers in
the pool, listening to the waves collapsing behind me, drinking Carta Blanca. The air stings my nose with exhaust fumes,
then salt. But I'm not in Mexico. I'm in Illinois, a bedroom,
standing beside an open drawer, pistol at my face, the smell of
oil. I run my fingers over the grooves beneath the barrel, the
matted handle. My tongue tastes the oil and metal of the small
opening. It tastes like pennies.

I sit back on the bed. The girl breathes heavily, rhyth-
mically. I straighten my legs on the bed, spread them, put the
gun between them on the sheet, just beneath my penis. I
twist to look again past the curtains, but the paved street, the
streetlamp, is gone.

In a village outside of Huan Fo, Olson stands, weight on
one leg, left hand stuffed in his pants pocket, right hand holding a wet clipboard and wrinkled sheets of paper, radio
strapped across a shoulder. He leans against the supply truck
tailgate, lifts the clipboard above his eyes, and stares off
into the drizzle. I squat beside Olson, partially protected
from the rain by the tailgate, M-16 between my legs. Carts
move through the rutted roads, wet, glistening animal backs.
People, bent and straight, hurry through the rain. "Truman
got fragged bad is the word," I say.

Olson looks down at my face, lifts the clipboard to the center of his helmet. "I heard not so bad."

"Could have been dead," I say.

"What's got you so morbid, Hagget?" Olson looks back out
at the village, thatched roofs slick with rain. Crane and Anderson backing out of one hut, laughing, hands over their eyes.
"How much longer?" Olson yells at them.

They both turn, smiling. Crane holds his stomach. Anderson moves his hands from his eyes to his mouth. "Crane's in love," Anderson yells back, white teeth, black face, brown eyes, khaki helmet. They laugh.

"How much longer?" Olson yells again.

They walk toward us. The misting rain thickens. Crane steps in puddles, Anderson hops and zags. "Be here the rest of the day," Anderson says. He reaches inside his helmet next to his ear, produces a cigarette. "If we're lucky." He squats, face level with mine, leans under the truck, and lights his cigarette. "Secret of smoking in the rain is just getting it started." He smiles at me, sucks hard. "The Oklahoma Crane's in love. Be a Cranette in there." I smile so he won't go into detail. Crane's a virgin and the running joke's grown old. "You and Olson," Anderson says, pointing at the next hut. I stand. Olson gives Crane the clipboard and picks up his rifle.

In the hut, a pregnant woman sits on an army cot, smiling, belly like a party balloon, black hair knotted below her head. I rummage through her shallow shelves—half a pack of stale Marlboros, white thread, a pipe that looks hand-carved. Olson lifts a corner of the webbed mat off the floor. The woman smiles, nods. Water trickles down the wall I'm facing. A photograph. "Look at this," I say, and Olson drops the mat.

In the photograph the woman is thin, just a girl, arm around an American in fatigues, a car in the background, a brick building. "Saigon," the woman says, and we look at her. "Jin Coosaan," she says. "You know?" I shake my head. On the back of the photograph is *Love, Jim.*

We mull through her pots, rice, clothes. "Raining hard," Olson says, standing in the doorway watching it fall. The woman on the bed lies back. I look at her belly. Underneath the cot I see something metal. I flap the butt of my rifle against Olson's thigh and move toward the bed. Olson turns. She sits up quickly, smiles. I reach under the bed, she jumps forward, and Olson lets his rifle drop even with her head. She begins crying.

I move my hands cautiously under the bed, pull out a gray metal box with rounded corners and a flip latch. "Careful," Olson says, the rifle still at her head.

I turn the box around, flip open the latch, lift the lid slowly. Fishing gear. Flies, hooks, weights, line, a shiny reel. I turn the box to face me again. Inside, a piece of white tape has written on it *Jim Cousins* and an address in Sioux City. I close the box and slide it back under the bed. "Okay," I say to her. She smiles.

I stand at the door with Olson, watch the rain thicken until it seems to become something solid, standing upright, like a curtain of magnesium. I believe Olson sees the same thing, but he says, "Looks like smoke."

I look back at the curtain of magnesium, sometimes translucent, and the truck becomes visible, Crane and Anderson underneath the tailgate, sitting on their helmets, cigarettes glowing orange. Suddenly, somewhere behind the curtain, a rifle begins firing, then another. I see Anderson roll in the mud, trying to get behind the curtain, no, behind the truck. The curtain shifts, the truck becomes invisible, Crane and Anderson invisible. "They running?" It's Olson's voice. His M-16 is pointed out the door at the curtain.

"They might be," I say.

"Where's it coming from?"

I shake my head. "We shoot, they may fire over here."

I look back at the woman. She's lying on her side on the floor underneath the cot. Cupped in her arms, the tackle box. Another burst of fire. The roof trembles and creaks. We drop, flatten against the mat. Water falls across my legs from holes in the roof the size of half-dollars. The pregnant woman coughs a scream into her hand.

Linda muffles her own cry. One hand moves from her mouth to my thigh, the other to my shoulder. She's staring at the pistol on the bed, between my legs.

"It was Olson at the door," I say.

She moves her hand from my thigh to my penis. Her finger-tips touch the pistol.

"He wants me to keep it for him."

She looks up at me, her eyes blank. "Why?"

I shake my head. "He trusts me."

"Is it loaded?"

I pick up the pistol, pull the clip. It slides silently out of the handle. Three bullets. "It's loaded," I say. I pop the clip back into the handle. Linda jumps, both her hands lift momentarily, then resettle against me. I stand, walk back to the open drawer, put the pistol under the T-shirts again.

"Did he shoot somebody, Hagget?"

I turn and look at her, sheet pulled up to her neck, her eyes on the drawer, then on me. "He said he did the right thing." I lie next to her. She holds me very tightly.

"What happened between you?" she asks.

"The war?"

She nods.

I start telling her about Saigon, a memory, but it wasn't really Saigon, it was Mexico, Mazatlán. I tell her Olson and I were walking, but it was just me on the curving sidewalk next to the beach, late in the evening. The street followed the curve of the ocean and behind the street were bars, restaurants, hotels, rent-a-cars, trinket shops, and, behind them, the city.

I tell her the traffic was thick, American cars, jeeps, thick noise and exhaust, but in Mazatlán the sound of the ocean muffled the noise, the wind off the water blew the exhaust inland. A boy ran across the street, just avoiding an old Chevy pickup. He was little, maybe ten, barefoot, dark hair, dark eyes, smiling a vaguely familiar smile. I tell her Olson pointed, but it was just me, looking at the boy, then back across the street to where he had run from. Another boy in green shorts and a pajama top took slow, careful steps toward a mound on the sidewalk. He extended his arm and touched the mound, then ran across the street to his friend, the same smile on his face—mischievous, knowing. I looked back at the mound, but I tell her that it was both of us looking, and that Olson said the mound was another little boy playing dead.

Linda sits up suddenly in the bed. "Was it a dead little boy?" she asks.

"A bus passed, blocking our view." I can see the bus, bright yellow lights above the windshield, thin driver in a gray suit and cap, ceramic Madonna dangling next to his head. I tell her we looked again after the bus passed, but it was only me, almost even with the boy, but it wasn't a boy, a woman, bare legs stretching into the street, head on the cracked cement, arms strewn over her face. She is at the base of an open-air restaurant. Above her a heavyset American in a checkered sportshirt says something to his wife, who is partially hidden behind an arch of red brick. He laughs, snaps his fingers for a waiter. They don't see the body, and I don't tell Linda about them or the restaurant.

"We waited for the traffic to clear, then crossed the street to the woman." Thin arms, knobby elbows crusted with black dirt. "Olson put his hand on her cheek." I put my hand on her cheek. Her cheek is cold, her neck stiff. "He turned her head to face us." Brown eyes open, locked, but they seem alive. "He took her pulse." I go to one knee, take her wrist. No pulse. I look again at her eyes. I bend closer. "She was dead." Across her iris move tiny flat insects.

Linda stares another moment, then kisses me lightly.

"I'll bury the gun," I say. "Tomorrow."

She nods, kisses me again. She rests her head on my chest.

The woman under the cot pulls the gray box up to her face. Water splatters on the cot into a pool. "Radio," I say, turning to Olson. "Tell them snipers. Village in trouble."

Another burst of fire. "*We're* in trouble," Olson says. He has the radio out. The rain slackens for a second, but I don't have the angle to see the truck. I hear Olson calling for cover, the woman crying, rain spitting through the roof. "They say clear out," Olson whispers, suddenly beside me on his belly.

"Where?" The rain is solid, the sky half an hour from darkness.

"Away from the fucking truck."

I nod, rise to my knees, crawl into the mud as fire sounds again and metallic punctures creak back an answer. "Away from the fucking truck," Olson repeats as he grabs my arm at the shoulder, pulling me up.

We run, rifles in our hands, thrashing through the curtain in front of us, mouths open for oxygen. Mud grips my boots. My right foot hits a deep puddle, I tumble, sweeping my rifle across the back of Olson's legs. "I'm hit," he yells. But I jump up, pull him forward, shaking my head, and he runs. I run. The curtain doesn't lift. We run blind in the rain.

Other Iowa Short Fiction Award Winners

1984
Old Wives' Tales,
Susan M. Dodd
Judge: Frederick Busch

1983
Heart Failure, Ivy Goodman
Judge: Alice Adams

1982
Shiny Objects, Dianne Benedict
Judge: Raymond Carver

1981
The Phototropic Woman,
Annabel Thomas
Judge: Doris Grumbach

1980
Impossible Appetites,
James Fetler
Judge: Francine du Plessix Gray

1979
Fly Away Home, Mary Hedin
Judge: John Gardner

1978
A Nest of Hooks, Lon Otto
Judge: Stanley Elkin

1977
The Women in the Mirror,
Pat Carr
Judge: Leonard Michaels

1976
The Black Velvet Girl,
C. E. Poverman
Judge: Donald Barthelme

1975
*Harry Belten and the
Mendelssohn Violin Concerto*,
Barry Targan
Judge: George P. Garrett

1974
*After the First Death There Is
No Other*, Natalie L. M. Petesch
Judge: William H. Gass

1973
The Itinerary of Beggars,
H. E. Francis
Judge: John Hawkes

1972
The Burning and Other Stories,
Jack Cady
Judge: Joyce Carol Oates

1971
*Old Morals, Small Continents,
Darker Times*,
Philip F. O'Connor
Judge: George P. Elliott

1970
The Beach Umbrella,
Cyrus Colter
Judges: Vance Bourjaily and
Kurt Vonnegut, Jr.